NOTE TO ADULTS

The recipes in this book are all suitable for children of 9 years and over, and many younger children will also enjoy the simple ones. As certain recipes require more advanced skills than others, each one is graded in the list of contents to show how difficult it is.

EXPLANATION OF SYMBOLS USED IN THE LIST OF CONTENTS

These are the easiest recipes and are ideal for beginners. Many of them require little or no cooking and are quick to prepare.

Most of the recipes in the book fall into this category. Many involve grating or chopping, as well as various types of cooking, except frying.

These are the most difficult recipes. Some involve frying. Others, such as those for decorated cakes, may have more complex instructions and demand a higher degree of patience and skill.

It is advisable for you to help children choose a recipe and be ready to assist them in the preparation of it. Some recipes involve frying and the use of sharp knives. It is important to read the recipes before your child starts cooking so that you know when help might be needed.

THE TEDDY BEAR COOK BOOK

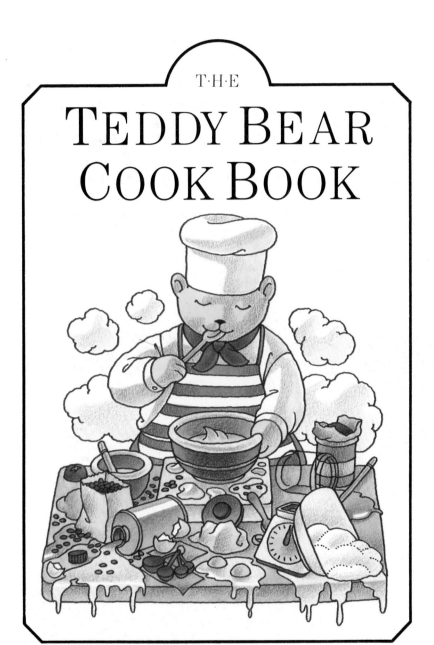

This edition first published 1991 by Dean, part of
Reed International Books Ltd., Michelin House, 81 Fulham Road,
London SW3 6RB.

Copyright © 1986 Octopus Books Limited

Illustrator Graham Percy

Photographer Graham Miller
Food prepared by Jane Miller
Stylist Pip Kelly

ISBN 0 603 55065 7

Produced by Resopal. Printed in Portugal.

T·H·E
TEDDY BEAR
COOK BOOK

LOUISE STEELE

DEAN

C·O·N·T·E·N·T·S

The Little Bears Show How Difficult The Recipes Are

Very easy

Fairly easy

More difficult

F·A·V·O·U·R·I·T·E · F·A·R·E

B·I·R·T·H·D·A·Y·S

E·A·S·T·E·R

P·I·C·N·I·C·S

B·A·R·B·E·C·U·E·S · A·N·D · H·A·L·L·O·W·E·E·N

P·R·E·S·E·N·T·S

C·H·R·I·S·T·M·A·S

F·U·N · F·O·O·D

S·I·P·S · A·N·D · S·O·D·A·S

I·N·T·R·O·D·U·C·T·I·O·N

The Teddy Bear Cook Book is a new collection of recipes, all devised specially for you to enjoy. There are recipes for summer and recipes for winter, and lots of unusual ideas for parties and presents, too. Whatever your own particular likes and dislikes, you can be sure that you will find plenty of delicious dishes and snacks that you will want to make time and time again!

We all know what you would find if you ever looked into a Teddy Bear's secret cupboard. So you won't be surprised that lots of the recipes in this cook book contain that special ingredient – HONEY!

Every Teddy Bear would agree that you can have too much of a good thing, even if it's honey. That's why this book includes recipes for savoury things as well as sweet things. Teddy Bears happen to be particularly fond of cakes, biscuits and sweets – but they know that to be fit and healthy and full of energy it's important to eat other things too. You will see that there are lots of recipes containing meat, fish, cheese, eggs, milk, vegetables and fruits – all great fun to make and mouth-watering to eat.

Cooking is as easy as A B C, providing you follow the recipes carefully each time. When you decide that you would like to do some cooking, don't rush into it. Have a good browse through the recipes and choose one that's

not too complicated for you. Make sure you have all the ingredients before you start and check that you've plenty of time. Some of the recipes in this cook book take only 15 minutes, but some take much longer. So always check the time involved, especially if you want to make something like jelly, which needs to set, or ice cream, which has to freeze. Not even the greediest Teddy Bears like sloppy jelly! They don't like burnt biscuits either, so never forget about things when they are in the oven!

We hope that this book will give you hours of fun and enjoyment, and lots of surprises too. There's something particularly satisfying about creating your own home-made goodies to share with your family and friends. Don't be afraid to try new foods and flavours – you'll never know what you've missed if you don't! After a while, when you've tried a recipe a few times, you'll find you have ideas of your own to make it even better.

Experimenting can be great fun, but it's usually a good idea to get advice from a more experienced cook before you do anything too adventurous!

So now take your pick from the treats that lie in store on the pages that follow.
Enjoy Yourself . . . Happy Cooking . . .
and Happy Eating Too!

BEFORE YOU BEGIN COOKING

1. Wash your hands.
2. Wear a clean apron.
3. Tie back long hair to keep it out of your eyes.

BE PREPARED

1. Make sure an adult is always with you during the preparation and cooking for a dish.

2. Carefully read through the recipe you have chosen before you start and make sure you understand it. If you are not sure about anything, ask an adult for advice.

3. Before you start, collect together all the utensils and equipment you need – you will find these listed at the beginning of each recipe.

4. Take care to measure out all the ingredients you need, making sure that they are accurate each time, otherwise the recipe may not work properly and you will be disappointed.

SAFETY FIRST

A good cook is always careful, so:

DON'T play in the kitchen – it can be very dangerous.
NEVER use a knife that is too big for you to handle easily. Always hold the handle of the knife firmly with one hand. Keep the fingers of your other hand (the one holding the food) well away from the blade of the knife.

Watch what you are doing all the time.
ALWAYS chop and slice ingredients on a chopping board.
NEVER use electrical appliances on your own.
NEVER touch electrical appliances, electric plugs or sockets with wet hands.
ALWAYS ask an adult to switch on the oven or grill.
DON'T rush to finish a recipe – accidents can happen this way. Take your time and follow the recipe carefully.
ALWAYS use oven gloves to protect your hands when putting dishes into the oven, or when taking hot dishes out of the oven.
ALWAYS stand back from a hot oven when you open the door, to prevent the hot air from burning your face.
ALWAYS hold a saucepan or frying pan handle when you are stirring or turning the contents.
ALWAYS make sure saucepan or frying pan handles are well away from other hot burners.
ALWAYS wipe up any spills on the floor – or you could slip and hurt yourself.
ALWAYS ask an adult to open cans of food for you.
NEVER attempt to open a corned beef or sardine can on your own.

HAPPY ENDINGS!

PLEASE leave the kitchen clean and tidy so that you will be allowed to have a cooking session another day.

REMEMBER to turn off the oven, grill and hot burners when you have finished cooking.

COOKING TERMS

You want to be sure of tasty results every time, so follow the methods given in the recipes very carefully. Below we explain some of the more usual basic cooking terms, so that you can refer to them when you need to.

Peeling Most vegetables and fruits need peeling before using. Use a potato peeler (it's safer than knife). Hold the vegetable tightly in one hand and over a plate to catch the peelings. It is safer to peel the vegetable toward you, turning it around as you go.

Grating Always put the base of the grater on a flat, non-slip surface, such as a chopping board or grate into a bowl standing on a damp cloth. Hold the item you are grating firmly in one hand and keep the fingertips of this hand tucked well away from the grating area. Hold the grater firmly with the other hand.

Chopping and Slicing Always use a chopping board and a sharp knife. To chop means to cut into small pieces or cubes, whereas to slice means to cut across to give even-sized slices.

Rubbing-in When you add fat to flour in pastry-making and for scones, rub with your fingertips and thumbs and keep lifting the ingredients slightly above the bowl until the mixture resembles fine breadcrumbs.

Kneading For bread and yeast recipes, the dough is kneaded with a strong pulling and stretching action. You must be much gentler when you make a pastry or biscuit dough – form the dough into a ball and put it on a lightly floured work surface. Using fingertips only, gently draw the outside of the dough to the centre, turning the dough ball in a clockwise direction as you go. Do this until the dough is smooth and free from cracks.

Combining, Mixing and Blending To mix ingredients well together until evenly blended, use either a spoon, fork or clean hands (depending on the recipe). In some cases an electric mixer or blender may also be used.

Creaming Most often used in cake-making, this simply means to soften and mix ingredients together (usually fat and sugar) until they are soft and fluffy-looking. Creaming is usually done with a wooden spoon.

Beating Used to mix ingredients together briskly, beating should be done with a wooden spoon to add air to the mixture for a light, well-risen result.

Folding You need to be light-handed and very gentle when folding one mixture into another. Always use a large metal spoon to cut through, lift and mix the ingredients together lightly but evenly. This method is used in meringue-making, when adding the sugar to the whisked egg whites.

Whisking Use a rotary hand whisk to beat air into a mixture such as cream or egg whites, to make the ingredients larger in volume and stiff enough to stand in peaks.

Rolling Before you start, lightly sprinkle a flat work surface and a rolling pin with plain flour – this is to prevent the dough from sticking. Roll the rolling pin across the surface of the dough in several short rolls, turning the dough when necessary.

A·T·A·S·T·E·O·F·H·O·N·E·Y

Teddy Bears love honey and who can blame them? It is so good to eat. Apart from enjoying honey as a delicious spread on fresh bread and butter or slices of toast, here are a few more tasty ways of enjoying this pure, natural food.

Spoon warmed honey over hot fritters and pancakes.

Mix a little honey with some melted chocolate and serve as a sauce over sponge puddings and ice cream.

Spread honey over grapefruit halves and grill until lightly golden.

Mix a little honey with freshly squeezed orange juice and use as a syrup for fresh fruit salads.

Use a little honey instead of sugar to sweeten your tea or coffee.

HONEY HINTS

If a jar of clear honey turns sugary, simply place the jar in a pan of hot, not boiling, water for a short time and it will become liquid again.

Clear honey pours more easily when warmed slightly, so when measuring honey in tablespoons, dip the spoon in hot water first and the honey will then slide easily off the spoon.

When measuring clear honey in a scale pan, very lightly grease the pan first and you will find the honey won't stick.

F·A·V·O·U·R·I·T·E · F·A·R·E

eddy Bears may not be renowned as athletes or gymnasts, but this doesn't mean that they never use up lots of energy. There are times when a busy bear feels like something warm and filling that's quick and easy to make. These recipes use some of their favourite foods like fish fingers, baked beans, jelly and yoghurt. They are not difficult to prepare and they will leave you with a pleasant well-fed feeling. Ideal for novice cooks, they will prove that you don't need to be a professional to produce some really nourishing food.

COWBOY HASH

Serves 4

INGREDIENTS	YOU WILL NEED
1 onion	knife, for chopping
1 potato	potato peeler
1 × 198 g (7 oz) can corned beef	chopping board
1 tablespoon corn oil	grater
1 × 225 g (7.94 oz) can	can opener
baked beans	tablespoon
100 g (4 oz) frozen peas	large frying pan
1 tablespoon tomato ketchup	wooden spoon
salt and pepper to taste	

Preparation time: 15 minutes
Cooking time: 15 minutes

1. Peel the onion and the potato. Now chop the onion and grate the potato (watch your hands!).
2. Ask an adult to open the corned beef can for you and cut the meat into chunky pieces. Put to one side.
3. Put the oil into a large frying pan and heat it gently until it is hot. Remove the pan from the heat.
4. Put the chopped onion and the grated potato into the pan. Fry them over a moderate heat for 5 minutes until they are soft but not brown, stirring frequently.
5. Add the baked beans, peas and tomato ketchup. Stir well and then add the corned beef. Add salt and pepper to taste and cook over a moderate heat for 8 minutes, stirring frequently. Serve hot with crusty bread.

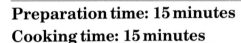

CHICK 'N' CORN FRIES

Serves 4 (makes 8)

INGREDIENTS	YOU WILL NEED
1 onion	knife, for chopping
175 g (6 oz) cooked chicken	chopping board
50 g (2 oz) plain flour, sifted	sieve
salt and pepper to taste	medium bowl
1 egg	wooden spoon
2 tablespoons milk	tablespoon
75 g (3 oz) sweetcorn niblets	large frying pan
2 tablespoons corn oil	fish slice

Preparation time: 15 minutes
Cooking time: 6-8 minutes

1. Peel and chop the onion and cut the chicken into small pieces.
2. Put the flour into a medium bowl. Sprinkle in the salt and pepper. Now crack the egg into the flour and add the milk.
3. Mix with a wooden spoon until the mixture is smooth. Now add the onion, chicken and sweetcorn and mix well.
4. Gently heat a tablespoon of the oil in a large frying pan. Place 4 rounded tablespoons of the mixture into the hot oil and flatten slightly with a fish slice.
5. Fry over a moderate heat for 3-4 minutes on one side, then carefully turn each one over, using the fish slice. Cook for a further 3-4 minutes until golden brown and cooked through.
6. One by one, carefully lift the Chick 'n' Corn Fries out of the frying pan, using the fish slice. Keep them warm while you cook the remaining mixture in the same way, using the second tablespoon of oil.
7. These are delicious served hot with tomato ketchup.

minutes until golden brown and cooked through.

5. Take the baking sheet out of the oven, using oven gloves. Leave to cool a little before eating.

QUICKIE PIZZA FACES

Makes 8

INGREDIENTS	YOU WILL NEED
2 carrots	grater
25 g (1 oz) butter or	plate
margarine, softened	medium bowl
2 tablespoons tomato or	fork
mild chilli relish	knife
100 g (4 oz) Cheddar cheese	serving plate
8 crumpets	
8 raisins or sultanas	
1 cocktail gherkin	
8 small cucumber wedges	

Preparation time: 15 minutes
Cooking time: 6-7 minutes

1. Grate the carrots and put to one side.
2. Put the butter or margarine into a bowl with the tomato or chilli relish.
3. Grate the Cheddar cheese (be careful not to grate your hands!) and put it in the bowl with the butter and relish. Now mix them together well with a fork.
4. Turn on the grill and let it warm up for a minute or so. Put the crumpets on the grill pan grid and grill them on both sides until they are a light golden colour.
5. Divide your mixture into 8 and place a portion on each crumpet. Press down with a knife to level.
6. Put the crumpets back under the grill for 3-4 minutes until the topping has melted and is lightly golden. Turn the grill off but leave the crumpets on the grid for the moment.
7. Now you can prepare the pizza faces. Take the crumpets off the grill pan grid and arrange them on a plate. Give each one a face, using the raisins or sultanas for eyes, small slices of gherkin for noses, and cucumber wedges for mouths. Use the grated carrot to give each crumpet some hair.

FISH SIZZLES

Makes 8

INGREDIENTS	YOU WILL NEED
a little oil, for greasing	pastry brush
8 frozen fish fingers	baking sheet
2 tablespoons tomato ketchup	plate
8 rashers boneless streaky bacon	scissors

Preparation time: 10 minutes
Cooking time: 25-30 minutes

1. Heat the oven to 190°C, 375°F, Gas Mark 5.
2. Lightly brush the baking sheet with oil. Brush each fish finger all over with tomato ketchup and put them on a plate.
3. Cut the rind off the bacon, using scissors. Wrap a rasher of bacon around each fish finger, winding it around from one end to the other.
4. Now transfer the bacon-wrapped fish fingers to a baking sheet and cook in the preheated oven for 25-30

HAM TWISTER SALAD

Serves 4

INGREDIENTS
water, as needed
100 g (4 oz) wholewheat
  pasta spirals or twists
1 onion
¼ cucumber
1 red eating apple
100 g (4 oz) sliced ham
50 g (2 oz) walnuts or peanuts
50 g (2 oz) raisins or sultanas
4 tablespoons mayonnaise
parsley to garnish

YOU WILL NEED
medium saucepan
colander
knife, for cutting
chopping board
large bowl
large metal spoon
serving bowl

Preparation time: 15 minutes
Cooking time: 15 minutes

1. Three-quarters fill the saucepan with water and bring to the boil. When the water is boiling, add the pasta shapes and boil, uncovered, for about 12 minutes, or until the pasta is tender. Drain carefully in a colander and then rinse the pasta in cold water to cool. Drain again and keep to one side.
2. Peel and chop the onion. Chop the cucumber and put it in the bowl with the onion. Cut the apple into quarters, remove the cores and chop. Add it to the onion and cucumber. Chop the ham and the nuts and put them in the mixing bowl. Now add the raisins.
3. Add the pasta shapes to the ingredients in the mixing bowl and stir them well with a spoon.
4. Pour in the dressing or mayonnaise and stir everything up together until all the ingredients are evenly mixed and coated in the dressing. Turn the mixture into a serving bowl. Garnish with parsley.

Left: Quickie Pizza Faces; Top: Fish Sizzles; Bottom: Ham Twister Salad

CREAMY FRUIT DESSERT

Serves 4

INGREDIENTS	YOU WILL NEED
1 small banana	knife, for cutting
1 ripe pear	chopping board
1 small red eating apple	medium bowl
6 strawberries	tablespoon
6 grapes	teaspoon
300 ml (½ pint) plain yoghurt	
2 tablespoons clear honey	

Preparation time: 15 minutes

1. Peel the banana and the pear. Cut the apple into quarters (but don't peel it) and remove the core. Now cut it into small pieces. Peel, core and chop the pear. Slice the banana neatly.
2. Remove any stalks or leaves from the strawberries. Slice 4 strawberries and keep 2 to one side. Cut each grape in half and take out the seeds (they taste bitter).
3. Put the yoghurt into a bowl and stir in the honey. Add all the prepared fruits and mix them in.
4. Spoon into glasses and top with half a strawberry.

Front: Creamy Fruit Dessert; Back: Peach Melba Whip

HONEY SWEET APPLES

Serves 4

INGREDIENTS	YOU WILL NEED
15 g (½ oz) butter or margarine, for greasing	shallow ovenproof dish
4 medium cooking apples	apple corer
4 tablespoons orange juice	chopping board
3 tablespoons clear honey	knife, for cutting
8 marshmallows	small saucepan
	tablespoon

Preparation time: 15 minutes
Cooking time: 45-50 minutes

1. Heat the oven to 190°C, 375°F, Gas Mark 5. Grease the shallow ovenproof dish with butter or margarine.
2. Take the cores out of the apples, but do not peel them. Put them on their sides on a board and cut a line, just through the skins, all the way round the centre.
3. Sit the apples on their stalk ends in the greased dish.
4. Heat the orange juice and honey together in the saucepan until they have melted, then spoon the syrup over the apples.
5. Put 4 marshmallows to one side for later. Cut the remaining 4 into quarters and push them into the middle of each apple.
6. Cook in the preheated oven for 45-50 minutes, spooning the liquid over the apples twice during the cooking.
7. Take the dish of apples out of the oven, using oven gloves. Top each apple with a marshmallow. Leave them to cool for a few minutes before serving.

HONEY BEARS' CRUMBLE

Serves 4-6

INGREDIENTS	YOU WILL NEED
a little butter, for greasing	pastry brush
2 cooking apples	1.1 litre (2 pint) shallow ovenproof dish
225 g (8 oz) fresh or frozen raspberries	knife, for cutting
2 teaspoons cornflour	2 medium bowls
2-3 tablespoons clear honey	tablespoon

Topping:
50 g (2 oz) hard margarine
75 g (3 oz) plain flour, sifted
50 g (2 oz) demerara sugar
50 g (2 oz) muesli

teaspoon
sieve

Preparation time: 20 minutes
Cooking time: 40-45 minutes

---

1. Heat the oven to 190°C, 375°F, Gas Mark 5. Lightly brush the ovenproof dish with a little butter.
2. Peel the cooking apples, cut them into quarters and then remove the core. Cut them into slices.
3. Now put the sliced apples and the raspberries together in a bowl. Sprinkle on the cornflour and add the honey. Mix them up together and turn the mixture into the ovenproof dish.
4. Cut the margarine into small pieces. Put the sifted flour into a mixing bowl and add the pieces of chopped margarine. Rub them together with your fingertips until the mixture looks like fine breadcrumbs. Now stir in the sugar and the muesli. When all the ingredients are mixed, spoon this topping mixture over the fruit. Use a spoon to level the surface.
5. Put the crumble into the preheated oven and cook for 40 minutes, or until the topping is golden brown and the fruit is cooked through. Cool a little before serving.

PEACH MELBA WHIP

Serves 4

INGREDIENTS	YOU WILL NEED
	scissors
1 × 135 g (4¾ oz) packet raspberry jelly	small saucepan
	measuring jug
150 ml (¼ pint) boiling water	can opener
	tablespoon
1 × 425 g (15 oz) can peach slices	sieve
	knife, for cutting
cold water, as needed	large bowl
150 ml (¼ pint) plain yoghurt	chopping board
	rotary hand whisk
150 ml (¼ pint) double cream	4 serving glasses

Preparation time: 15 minutes
Cooking time: 2-3 minutes
Setting time: 3½ hours

---

1. Cut the jelly into cubes, using the scissors, and put them in a small saucepan. Pour in the boiling water and stir over a low heat until the jelly has dissolved. Pour the liquid into a measuring jug.
2. Drain the peach slices and pour the juice onto the dissolved jelly. Add enough cold water to measure 600 ml (1 pint) altogether and stir it in.
3. Leave the jelly in the refrigerator for 1-1½ hours until it begins to set slightly and is soft and wobbly.
4. Meanwhile you can chop up the peach slices.
5. When the jelly is ready, turn it into a large bowl. Add the yoghurt and whisk them together with the rotary hand whisk until combined. Stir in the chopped peaches, reserving 4 pieces for decoration.
6. Spoon the mixture into 4 serving glasses and put them in the refrigerator to set for at least 2 hours.
7. When you are ready, whisk the cream until it forms soft peaks. Spoon it over the jellies, top with peach.

B·I·R·T·H·D·A·Y·S

Teddy Bears can always find an excuse for celebrating. They love parties. You will even catch them on the dance floor, providing there are plenty of savoury bites waiting for them afterwards – and something sweet and sticky to follow. Birthdays are a great time for having a party and making some special snacks and cakes. There are lots of tempting recipes to choose from here, including two scrumptious cakes to be the centrepiece of your birthday spread. You'll have fun making the Ring o' Roses Cake and the Party Express – and you'll have fun eating them too!

HAM AND COLESLAW CRUNCH

Makes 4

INGREDIENTS	YOU WILL NEED
8 slices Granary bread	chopping board
100 g (4 oz) full fat soft cheese	knife, for spreading
4 slices ham	knife, for cutting
100 g (4 oz) coleslaw	
¼ cucumber	

Preparation time: 15 minutes

1. Spread the slices of bread on one side with cheese.
2. Arrange a slice of ham on 4 slices of bread.
3. Top each one with the coleslaw and spread it out.
4. Slice the cucumber and arrange on the coleslaw.
5. Place the remaining slices of bread, cheese side down, on each one and press lightly.
6. Cut each sandwich into quarters.

BURGER RELISH BOATS

Serves 4

INGREDIENTS	YOU WILL NEED
1 large onion	baking sheet
40 g (1½ oz) soft margarine	sharp knife
1 tablespoon tomato, sweetcorn or mild chilli relish	chopping board
	small bowl
2 teaspoons corn oil	wooden spoon
6 fresh or frozen beefburgers	teaspoon
4 long crusty rolls	frying pan
8 slices tomato	fish slice
8 slices cucumber	plate
To serve:	bread board
mustard and cress or shredded lettuce	knife, for spreading
	large piece of foil
	serving plate

Preparation time: 20 minutes
Cooking time: 20 minutes

1. Heat the oven to 190°C, 375°F, Gas Mark 5. Make sure you have a baking sheet ready. Now peel the onion, slice it and separate it into rings, and put to one side.
2. Mix the margarine and the relish together in a small bowl and set the mixture to one side for the moment.
3. Heat the oil in the frying pan and add the beefburgers. Cook them over a moderate heat for 3 minutes, turning them over once. Add the onion rings and fry them for 2 more minutes. (Be careful not to let the onions burn.) When the onions are soft, transfer the beefburgers and the onions to a plate, using a fish slice.
4. Cut the rolls lengthways along the centre of the tops, cutting almost down to the bottom crust, but don't cut right through. Open each roll apart and spread the margarine and relish mixture inside and over the tops.
5. Put the rolls on a large piece of foil. Now cut the beefburgers in half and arrange 3 pieces in each roll. Add a few onion rings to each one.
6. Wrap the foil around all the rolls to cover them completely and place the foil parcel on a baking sheet. Cook in the preheated oven for 10 minutes and then take the baking sheet out of the oven. Keep your oven gloves on and fold back the foil so that the tops of the rolls are uncovered. Return them to the oven for 5 more minutes to crisp up.
7. When the tops are crisp, take the baking sheet out of the oven, using oven gloves. Add the slices of tomato and cucumber to each roll and arrange them on a serving plate with mustard and cress or shredded lettuce.

PARTY-TIME TWISTS

Makes 24

INGREDIENTS
50 g (2 oz) Cheddar cheese
a little flour, for
  sprinkling
1 × 227 g (8 oz) packet
  frozen puff pastry,
  thawed
2 teaspoons meat and
  yeast extract
beaten egg, to glaze

YOU WILL NEED
baking sheet
grater
plate
rolling pin
knife
teaspoon
pastry brush
wire rack

Preparation time: 20 minutes
Cooking time: 15 minutes

1. Heat the oven to 190°C, 375°F, Gas Mark 5. Have a baking sheet ready. Grate the cheese onto a plate.
2. Lightly sprinkle a work surface and rolling pin with flour. Roll out the thawed pastry thinly to make a rectangle measuring about 30 × 23 cm (12 × 9 inches).
3. Mark the rectangle in half lengthways (but don't cut!). Spread one half with the meat and yeast extract, leaving a border of 5 mm (¾ inch) around the edges.

4. Sprinkle the same area with grated cheese and pat it down. Brush lightly around the edges with water.
5. Now fold the plain half over the part with the filling and press the edges together very firmly to seal them.
6. Run a rolling pin gently over the surface of the pastry to flatten it slightly.
7. Brush the surface with beaten egg to glaze and then cut it into 24 strips, each about 10 mm (½ inch) wide.
8. Give each strip of pastry a twist and arrange them on a dampened baking sheet.
9. Cook the twists in a preheated oven for 15 minutes until they are golden brown and cooked through.
10. Put your oven gloves on to remove the baking sheet from the oven. Transfer the Party-Time Twists to a wire rack and leave them to cool before serving.

SANDWICH SWIRLS

Makes 24

INGREDIENTS
4 slices brown bread, ready-cut
4 slices white bread, ready-cut
50 g (2 oz) soft margarine
½ × 75 g jar sardine and
  tomato paste
½ box mustard and cress

YOU WILL NEED
bread board
bread knife
rolling pin
knife, for spreading
tablespoon
plastic wrap

Preparation time: 20 minutes
Chilling time: 1 hour

1. Place the bread on a board and cut off all the crusts. Flatten each slice by running a rolling pin over it.

2. Spread one side of each slice of bread with margarine, keeping a little margarine until later.

3. Spread the brown slices with most of the sardine and tomato paste and sprinkle them with mustard and cress.

4. Place the slices of white bread, buttered side down, on top of the sardine mixture. Press together firmly. Spread the top side of white bread with the margarine and paste you have left.

5. Roll up each sandwich really firmly, like a Swiss roll. Now fold the plastic wrap around them very tightly and put them in the refrigerator for 1 hour.

6. Remove the plastic wrap and cut each roll into 6 pinwheels. Arrange them neatly on a plate to serve.

STRAWBERRY CREAMS

Serves 4-6

INGREDIENTS	YOU WILL NEED
450 g (1 lb) fresh strawberries	fork
	plate
150 ml (¼ pt) double cream	2 medium bowls
150 ml (¼ pt) canned custard	rotary hand whisk
2-3 tablespoons icing sugar	large metal spoon
To decorate:	can opener
a few strawberries	
dainty, crisp biscuits	

Preparation time: 20 minutes

1. Mash the strawberries with a fork on a plate until you have a fairly smooth mixture and put it into a bowl.

2. Spoon the cream into another bowl and whisk it until the cream stands in stiff peaks.

3. Lightly stir the custard into the cream and then add to the strawberries. Add the icing sugar and stir the ingredients until they are evenly combined.

4. Spoon the mixture into serving dishes and decorate each one with a whole strawberry. Serve with dainty crisp biscuits.

ICE CREAM DREAMS

Serves 2

INGREDIENTS	YOU WILL NEED
2 ring doughnuts	2 serving plates
2 slices canned pineapple	can opener
2 scoops ice cream	ice cream scoop
a little strawberry dessert sauce, to taste	teaspoon
2 teaspoons chopped mixed nuts	

Preparation time: 5-10 minutes

1. Put the ring doughnuts onto 2 serving plates.

2. Top each one with a slice of pineapple.

3. Put a scoop of ice cream on each one and drizzle over a little strawberry dessert sauce, to taste.

4. Sprinkle with chopped nuts and serve.

PARTY EXPRESS

INGREDIENTS
1 slab of Angel cake
1 large jam-filled Swiss
  roll
a little jam, for spreading
100 g (4 oz) soft margarine
150 g (5 oz) icing sugar
3 teaspoons cocoa
4 chocolate mini Swiss
  rolls
a selection of liquorice
  allsorts
4 chocolate coins, covered
  in gold foil
jelly tots
liquorice strips or laces
small lollipops

YOU WILL NEED
bread knife
sharp knife
knife, for spreading
large silver board,
  (or foil-covered
  bread board)
medium bowl
wooden spoon
fork
cake candles and holders

Preparation time: 45 minutes

1. Cut off a 2.5 cm (1 inch) slab of Angel cake. You need a piece about 15 cm (6 inches) long and about 7.5 cm (3 inches) wide.
2. Put the slice of cake on to a silver board or foil-covered bread board. Spread the underside of the large Swiss roll with jam and stick it on to the Angel cake.
3. Put the margarine, icing sugar and cocoa into a bowl and mix well with a wooden spoon until soft and fluffy.
4. Carefully spread the icing over the Swiss roll and the Angel cake so that all the cake that shows is covered. Lightly fork up the icing to make it look pretty.
5. Cut 1 chocolate Swiss roll into 2 pieces, one slightly longer than the other. Put these on top of the Swiss roll to form funnels.
6. Place a whole chocolate Swiss roll on its side across the top of the engine, at the back, to form the cabin.
7. Decorate the sides of the engine with coconut liquorice allsorts and chocolate coins (covered in gold foil) to form wheels.
8. Decorate the Swiss roll with square liquorice allsorts for windows and put a blue liquorice allsort at the front.

Party Express

9. Using a little jam, stick 2 coconut liquorice allsorts and 2 liquorice logs to the top of the funnels to form chimney pots.

10. To make the 2 trucks, cut off 2 pieces of Angel cake from the slab, each one measuring about 5 cm (2 inches) wide and 7.5 cm (3 inches) long.

11. Coat these pieces of cake with butter icing and press a chocolate mini Swiss roll on top of each one. Lightly fork the icing to give a pretty effect.

12. Arrange the 2 trucks on the silver board, placing them at an angle, as shown in the photograph.

13. Decorate the trucks with coconut liquorice allsorts to form wheels and put jelly tots around the bases of the mini Swiss rolls. Put a pink liquorice allsort at the front.

14. Cut the liquorice strips into lengths and lay them out to make the railway tracks.

15. Stick candles (in candle holders) into the first truck and lollipops into the second truck.

ROBOT CAKES

Makes 6

INGREDIENTS	YOU WILL NEED
a little oil, for greasing	pastry brush
50 g (2 oz) self-raising flour, sifted	6 dariol moulds baking sheet
¼ teaspoon baking powder, sifted	sieve medium bowl
50 g (2 oz) soft margarine	teaspoon
50 g (2 oz) soft light brown sugar	wooden spoon grater
finely grated rind of ½ lemon	round-bladed knife wire rack
1 egg	sharp knife
To finish:	tablespoon
3 tablespoons lemon curd	small saucepan
3-4 tablespoons dessicated coconut	plate
6 jaffa cakes	
6 marshmallows	
3 glacé cherries, halved	
6 chocolate sticks	

Preparation time: 25-30 minutes
Cooking time: 20 minutes

1. Heat the oven to 200°C, 400°F, Gas Mark 6. Using a pastry brush, grease the base and sides of 6 dariol moulds and stand them on a baking sheet.

2. Put the sifted flour and baking powder into a medium bowl. Add the margarine, sugar, grated lemon rind and the egg.

3. Using a wooden spoon, mix the ingredients together until well combined and creamy.

4. Divide the mixture between the greased moulds and cook in the preheated oven for about 15 minutes until risen and cooked through.

5. Using oven gloves, remove baking sheet from the oven. Leave to cool for 5 minutes.

6. Run a round-bladed knife around the tins and turn out the cakes. Leave to cool on a wire rack.

7. Level off the wider ends of the buns.

8. Put the lemon curd into a small saucepan and place over a gentle heat, stirring, until melted. Remove from heat and brush over the bases and sides of buns.

9. Put the coconut on to a plate. Roll the buns in coconut until evenly coated.

10. Using a little melted lemon curd, stick the buns, wide sides down, onto the chocolate side of a jaffa cake.

11. Put a marshmallow on top of each one, using melted lemon curd to stick. Press half a glacé cherry on top.

12. Push a chocolate stick into each cake, between the marshmallow and cake.

RING-O-ROSES CAKE

INGREDIENTS
a little oil, for greasing
a little flour, for dusting
175 g (6 oz) self-raising
  flour, sifted
½ teaspoon baking
  powder, sifted
175 g (6 oz) caster sugar
175 g (6 oz) soft margarine
3 eggs
Icing:
275 g (10 oz) icing sugar, sifted
2-3 drops red food
  colouring
9-10 teaspoons water
To decorate:
jellied sweets
angelica
8 chocolate bunnies

YOU WILL NEED
pastry brush
23 cm (9 inch) diameter
  ring tin
sieve
teaspoon
large bowl
wooden spoon
knife
baking sheet
wire rack
medium bowl
large plate
silver board or serving
  plate

Left: Ring-o-Roses Cake; Right: Robot Cakes (p.21)

Preparation time: 30 minutes
Cooking time: 25-30 minutes

1. Heat the oven to 190°C, 375°F, Gas Mark 5. Lightly brush the base and sides of the cake tin with oil. Dust the inside with a little flour, shaking the tin to coat it evenly. Now turn the tin upside down and shake out the excess flour.

2. Put the sifted flour, baking powder, sugar, margarine and eggs into a large bowl. Beat well with a wooden spoon for 2 minutes until all the ingredients are blended and smooth. (If you are using an electric mixer, only beat for 1 minute, and remember to ask an adult to help you to use the machine.)

3. Spoon the mixture into the prepared tin and level the surface with a knife. Place the tin on a baking sheet and cook in the preheated oven for 25-30 minutes until it has risen and cooked through.

4. Put on your oven gloves and remove the cake from the oven. Leave it to cool in the tin for 10 minutes, then turn it out on to a wire rack and leave it to cool

thoroughly. (Ask an adult to help you to turn the cake out.)

5. When the the cake is cold, prepare the icing. Put the icing sugar and the colouring into a medium bowl. Add the water and mix well with a wooden spoon to make a smooth icing that coats the back of the spoon. (Ask an adult to check this for you.)

6. Place the cake on a wire rack over a large plate – this is to catch the icing that drips off.

7. Spoon the icing over the cake to coat it completely, spooning up the icing that falls on to the plate and using it to coat again.

8. Transfer the cake to a silver board or serving plate, using a fish slice and palette knife. (Ask an adult to help you do this.)

9. Decorate the top of the cake with 8 flowers, each one made of 5 jellied sweets. Decorate the side of the cake with 8 more flowers, using more coloured stars.

10. Cut the angelica into 8 thin stalks and 16 dainty leaf shapes and use these to decorate the flowers on the side of the cake.

11. Place a chocolate bunny between each flower on the side of the cake and press on lightly to make sure they stick firmly.

12. Leave the cake to set completely before serving.

CHOCOLATE BUTTERFLY BUNS

Makes 12

INGREDIENTS	YOU WILL NEED
90 g (3½ oz) self-raising flour, sifted	12 paper bun cases
1 teaspoon baking powder, sifted	bun tray (for 12 buns)
15 g (½ oz) cocoa, sifted	sieve
100 g (4 oz) soft margarine	teaspoon
100 g (4 oz) caster sugar	medium bowl
2 eggs	wooden spoon
Filling:	dessertspoon
150 ml (¼ pint) double cream	wire rack
	small knife, for cutting
	rotary hand whisk

To decorate:
12 small orange jelly slices
12 small lemon jelly slices

Preparation time: 25 minutes
Cooking time: 12-15 minutes

1. Heat the oven to 200°C, 400°F, Gas Mark 6. Put 12 paper cases in the bun tray.

2. Put the sifted flour, baking powder and cocoa into a medium bowl. Add the margarine, sugar and eggs.

3. Beat well with a wooden spoon for about 2 minutes until all the ingredients are blended and smooth. (If you are using an electric mixer, only beat the mixture for 1 minute, and remember to ask an adult to help you.)

4. Put heaped dessertspoonfuls of the mixture into the 12 paper cases in the tin, making sure you use up all the mixture by putting an equal amount in each paper case.

5. Cook in a preheated oven for 12-15 minutes until well risen and cooked through.

6. Remove the bun tray from the oven, using oven gloves, and leave the buns to cool in the tin for a few minutes. Transfer them to a wire rack to cool completely.

7. Slice off the tops of the cold cakes with a knife. Cut the tops in half and keep them to use later for wings.

8. Put the cream into a medium bowl and whisk until it stands in stiff peaks. Put a heaped teaspoonful of cream onto each cake and spread it out to cover the cut part of the cake.

9. Arrange the sliced tops to make 2 wings on top of each cake and decorate with 2 orange or lemon slices to make smaller wings.

E·A·S·T·E·R

eddy Bears always spring to life when Easter comes. It's the time of year when flowers begin to bud and trees look green and leafy again. Everything seems fresh and new. Teddy Bears are also fond of Easter because they know it means lots of favourite things from the kitchen: delicious Hot Cross Buns, piping hot from the oven, and – best of all – Easter eggs (you never know what you'll find inside!). Now you can try your hand at making your own Easter eggs. For a breakfast surprise, try the colourful Rainbow Eggs – you can eat them when you have displayed them on the table.

HOT CROSS BUNS

Makes 12

INGREDIENTS	YOU WILL NEED
a little oil, for greasing	pastry brush
1 × 280 g (10 oz) packet	baking sheet
white bread mix (with	large bowl
active yeast)	teaspoon
75 g (3 oz) dried mixed fruit	tablespoon
1 teaspoon mixed spice	measuring jug
200 ml (7 fl oz) tepid water	wooden spoon
a little beaten egg, to glaze	sheet of oiled
a little flour, for sprinkling	plastic wrap
a little caster sugar, for sprinkling	sharp knife
100 g (4 oz) marzipan	rolling pin
2 tablespoons clear honey	

Preparation time: 25 minutes
Cooking time: 20-22 minutes
Rising and proving time: 2½ hours

1. Using a pastry brush, grease a baking sheet with oil.
2. Put the bread mix into a large bowl. Add the fruit and spice and stir well. Add the tepid water and mix with a wooden spoon to form a dough.
3. Turn the dough onto a lightly floured work surface and knead for 10 minutes by hand until smooth.
4. Place the dough in the bowl, cover with lightly oiled plastic wrap, and leave to rise at room temperature for 1½-2 hours, or until it has doubled in size.
5. Turn the dough out onto a lightly floured surface and knead for 2-3 minutes. Divide the dough into 12 equal parts and shape each one into a round bun.
6. Place the buns on the baking sheet and cover them with a sheet of lightly oiled plastic wrap and leave to double in size at room temperature. This takes 30-40 minutes. Heat the oven to 190°C, 375°F, Gas Mark 5.
7. Brush the buns lightly with beaten eggs to glaze. Cook in the preheated oven for 15 minutes.
8. While the buns are cooking, prepare the marzipan crosses. Sprinkle a work surface with a little caster sugar. Roll out the marzipan to a 15 cm (6 inch) square. Trim the edges to neaten and cut into 12 equal strips.

Cut each strip in half to give 24 shorter strips.
9. Remove the baking sheet of buns from the oven after 15 minutes cooking time, using oven gloves. Arrange 2 strips in a cross over each bun and return to the oven.
10. Cook for a further 5-6 minutes until the buns are cooked through and lightly golden. Using oven gloves, remove the baking sheet from the oven.
11. Brush honey over the surface of the buns. Leave them to cool on a wire rack.

FLUFFY ORANGE DRINK

Serves 4

INGREDIENTS	YOU WILL NEED
2 × 150 ml (¼ pint)	blender goblet
mandarin yoghurts	measuring jug
300 ml (½ pint) orange	ice cream scoop
juice, unsweetened	sharp knife
4 large scoops vanilla ice	4 medium glasses
cream	straws
150 ml (¼ pint) fizzy	
lemonade or ginger ale	
4 orange slices	

Preparation time: 5 minutes

1. Place the yoghurt, orange juice and ice cream in a blender goblet. Make sure the lid is put on tightly.
2. Switch on blender and blend for 30-45 seconds until the mixture is smooth and frothy.
3. Pour the drink into 4 medium glasses and top up each one with fizzy lemonade or ginger ale.
4. Decorate the rim of each glass with a slice of orange. Serve at once with straws.

EGGY POTATO NESTS

Makes 4

INGREDIENTS
a little oil, for greasing
50 g (2 oz) Cheddar cheese
500 ml (28 fl oz) water
1 × 131 g packet of instant
  mashed potato
25 g (1 oz) butter or hard
  margarine
salt and pepper to taste
1 egg
Filling:
2 eggs, beaten
1 tablespoon milk
2 slices ham
50 g (2oz) cooked peas
salt and pepper to taste

YOU WILL NEED
pastry brush
baking sheet
grater
plate
saucepan
fork
small bowl
knife
teaspoon
rotary hand whisk
small saucepan
wooden spoon
fish slice

Preparation time: 20 minutes
Cooling time: 30 minutes
Cooking time: 30 minutes

1. Heat the oven to 200°C, 400°F, Gas Mark 6. Lightly brush the baking sheet with the oil.
2. Grate the cheese onto a plate and put it to one side.
3. Pour the water into a saucepan and bring to the boil. Remove the pan from the heat and sprinkle in the potato, ensuring the potato is covered with water.
4. Stir well with a fork, then add half the butter or margarine and all the grated cheese. Add salt and pepper to taste and mix well until thoroughly combined. Leave to cool for 30 minutes.
5. Crack 1 egg into a small bowl and beat with a fork. Add the beaten egg to the potato mixture and mix well together. Divide the mixture into 4 equal portions.
6. Place the portions of potato on the greased baking sheet. Use a knife to form them into 4 rounds, 10 cm (4 inches) across. Make a hollow in the centre of each one with a teaspoon to make them look like nests.
7. Fluff up the sides and top edge of each round with a fork. Cook in a preheated oven for 25-30 minutes until

golden brown and cooked through.
8. Wait until 10 minutes before the end of the cooking time and then prepare the scrambled egg mixture. Whisk the 2 eggs and milk together in a bowl, then stir in the ham, peas and salt and pepper to taste.
9. In a small saucepan, melt the remaining butter or margarine. When the fat is melted, stir the egg mixture into the pan and cook over a gentle heat for 3-4 minutes, stirring all the time with a wooden spoon until the mixture begins to set, but is still soft and creamy. Remove from the heat.
10. Remove the baking sheet from the oven, using oven gloves. Fill the hollows in the potato nests with the scrambled egg mixture. Use a fish slice to transfer the potato nests to serving plates. Serve hot.

SUNSHINE PLATTER

Serves 4

INGREDIENTS
1 onion
3 rashers streaky bacon
4 tablespoons corn oil
100 g (4 oz) long-grain rice
150 ml (¼ pint) boiling
  water
½ chicken stock cube,
  crumbled
150 ml (¼ pint) tomato
  juice
salt and pepper to taste
175 g (6 oz) frozen mixed
  vegetables (to include sweetcorn)
8 frozen fish fingers

YOU WILL NEED
tablespoon
wooden spoon
large saucepan
measuring jug
sharp knife
scissors

Preparation time: 20-25 minutes
Cooking time: 30 minutes

1. Peel and chop the onion and cut the bacon into small pieces. Heat 2 tablespoons of the oil in a large saucepan. Add the onion, bacon and rice and fry over a low heat for 3 minutes, stirring with a wooden spoon.
2. Very carefully stir in the boiling water, crumbled stock cube and tomato juice. Bring to the boil, then stir and add salt and pepper to taste. Cover the pan with a lid and cook gently for 10 minutes.
3. Remove the lid from the pan and add the frozen mixed vegetables. Stir well, then re-cover and cook for a further 12 minutes.
4. Meanwhile, brush the fish fingers lightly with the remaining oil and place on a grill pan grid. Cook under a medium hot grill for 10-12 minutes, turning once during cooking. Use oven gloves to protect your hands.
5. Stir the savoury rice, then arrange the rice in a mountain shape on a round plate. Place the fish fingers around the rice, radiating out like the face of a sun. Serve hot.

CHOCOLATE CREAM BUNNY

Serves 4-6

INGREDIENTS
1 × 600 ml (1 pint) packet chocolate blancmange powder
2 tablespoons granulated sugar
600 ml (1 pint) milk
25 g (1 oz) plain chocolate, grated
To decorate:
40 g (1½ oz) shredded coconut
a few drops of green food colouring
150 ml (¼ pt) double cream

YOU WILL NEED
medium bowl
tablespoon
wooden spoon
medium saucepan
600 ml (1 pint) bunny mould (or fluted jelly mould)
grater
plastic bag
serving plate
teaspoon

Preparation time: 20-25 minutes
Cooking time: 3 minutes
Setting time: several hours

1. Put the blancmange powder into a medium bowl. Add the sugar and just 2 tablespoons of the milk, taken from the 600 ml (1 pint).
2. Stir with a wooden spoon until smooth and creamy.
3. Put the remaining milk into a medium saucepan and heat until hot and bubbles appear on the surface, but do not let the milk boil.
4. Carefully pour the hot milk onto the blancmange mixture, stirring all the time with a wooden spoon. Pour the mixture back into the saucepan and bring to the boil, stirring all the time. Boil for 2 minutes until the mixture has thickened, still stirring.
5. Fill the jelly mould with cold water and empty the water away, but leave the mould damp. Quickly grate the chocolate into the hot blancmange (do *not* stir until it is completely dissolved).
6. Pour the hot blancmange mixture into the wet mould and leave it to cool for at least 45 minutes.
7. When the mixture is cool, place the mould in the refrigerator and leave for several hours to set.
8. Meanwhile, prepare the coconut grass to decorate. Put the shredded coconut into a plastic bag. Add 2 or 3 drops of green food colouring, then close up the bag.
9. Squeeze and rub the bag between your hands to colour the coconut green. Keep the coconut in the bag.
10. To serve: (Ask an adult to help you do this.) Place a serving plate over the top of the jelly mould. Turn them upside down together. Now lift off the mould.
11. Whip the cream until it forms stiff peaks and use a teaspoon to spoon it all around the blancmange.
12. Scatter the coconut grass around the cream.

MINI CHOCOLATE EGGS

Makes 8

INGREDIENTS
½ × 200 g packet plain
  chocolate flavour cake
  covering
100 g (4 oz) marzipan
dolly mixtures, liquorice
  allsorts or walnut halves,
  to decorate

YOU WILL NEED
heatproof medium bowl
medium saucepan
wooden spoon
knife
sheet of greaseproof paper
2 teaspoons
small paper sweet cases

Preparation time: 30 minutes
Cooking time: 5 minutes

1. Break the cake covering into small pieces. Put the pieces into a heatproof bowl, standing over a saucepan of hot (not boiling) water. Leave this to melt, then stir until smooth. Remove from heat.
2. While cake covering is melting, cut the marzipan into 8 equal pieces. Roll each one into a ball between the palms of your hands, then shape them into eggs.
3. Place a sheet of greaseproof paper on a flat surface.
4. Using a teaspoon, or 2 if you find it easier, drop each marzipan egg into the melted cake covering and turn until it is completely covered with chocolate.
5. Lift the egg from the chocolate and allow excess chocolate to drain off, then place the egg on the sheet of greaseproof paper. Leave to set for 5 minutes. Coat the remaining marzipan eggs in the same way.

Rainbow Eggs (p.31) and (middle) Mini Chocolate Eggs

6. Coat each egg once again in the melted chocolate. Leave to set on the greaseproof paper. This takes about 5 minutes.

7. Dip the tip of a knife into the remaining melted chocolate and spread a tiny amount onto one side of each sweet or nut being used and press lightly onto the set eggs. Leave for 15 minutes until hard and completely set.

8. Using a small knife, lift the chocolate eggs from the greaseproof paper. Cut away the excess chocolate from around the base of each egg and arrange each one in a pretty paper sweet case.

NOTE: If the cake covering begins to set in the bowl, place it over a saucepan of hot (not boiling) water.

EASTER BONNET BUNS

Makes 12

INGREDIENTS	YOU WILL NEED
100 g (4 oz) self-raising flour, sifted	12 paper bun cases
1 teaspoon baking powder, sifted	1 bun tray (for 12 buns)
	sieve
100 g (4 oz) caster sugar	medium bowl
100 g (4 oz) soft tub margarine (straight from the refrigerator)	teaspoon
	wooden spoon
	dessertspoon
2 eggs	wire rack
To decorate:	tablespoon
75 g (3 oz) soft tub margarine	fork
	knife, for spreading
100 g (4 oz) icing sugar, sifted	
1 tablespoon cocoa powder	
2 teaspoons milk	
2 tablespoons shredded coconut	
2 tablespoons chocolate flavour strands	
dainty sweets	

Preparation time: 25 minutes
Cooking time: 25 minutes

1. Heat the oven to 180°C, 350°F, Gas Mark 4. Place 12 paper bun cases in the bun tray.

2. Put the sifted flour and the baking powder into a medium mixing bowl (or use an electric food mixer, if you would prefer, but ask an adult to show you how).

3. Add the sugar, margarine and eggs and beat well with a wooden spoon for 2-3 minutes. (If you are using an electric mixer, mix for only 1 minute until mixture is soft and fluffy.)

4. Using a dessertspoon, place heaped spoonfuls of the mixture into each bun case.

5. Cook in a preheated oven for 25 minutes until well risen and cooked through. Protect your hands with oven gloves and remove bun tray from the oven. Lift the buns onto a wire rack and leave to cool for 30 minutes.

6. While the buns are cooling, prepare the icing. Put the margarine, icing sugar, cocoa and milk into a medium mixing bowl and mix well together with a fork until soft and well combined.

7. Using a knife, spread the icing over the top of the cold buns. Sprinkle 6 buns with shredded coconut and the other 6 buns with the chocolate strands. Press coconut and strands onto buns firmly to stick.

8. Decorate the buns with lots of little sweets.

HONEY SHAPES

Makes 12

INGREDIENTS

A little oil, for greasing

100 g (4 oz) butter or hard
  margarine, softened

50 g (2 oz) soft light brown sugar

2 tablespoons clear honey

1 egg

½ teaspoon finely grated
  lemon rind

225 g (8 oz) plain white
  flour, sifted

extra flour, for sprinkling

Icing:

100 g (4 oz) icing sugar, sifted

2½-3 teaspoons cold water

To decorate:

36 silver balls

YOU WILL NEED

pastry brush

2 baking sheets

medium bowl

wooden spoon

tablespoon

grater

fork

rolling pin

man and woman
  gingerbread cutters

wire rack

small bowl

palette knife

spoon

Preparation time: 30 minutes

Chilling time: 15 minutes

Cooking time: 15 minutes (for each baking sheet)

1. Preheat the oven to 180°C, 350°F, Gas Mark 4.
Lightly brush 2 baking sheets with the oil.
2. Put the butter or margarine, sugar and honey into a
bowl and mix well with a wooden spoon until soft.
3. Beat the egg and add it a little at a time, mixing well
after each addition.
4. Stir in the lemon rind and sifted flour and, using a
fork at first, mix well until evenly combined, then mix
by hand to form a dough.
5. Mould by hand until smooth and chill for 15 minutes.
6. Sprinkle a work surface and rolling pin with flour.
Roll out the dough to just under 5 mm (¼ inch) thick.
7. Using a gingerbread cutter, cut out 6 men, pressing
the cutter firmly into the rolled-out dough each time to
cut through the mixture.
8. Using a palette knife, lift the biscuits onto one of the

Left to right clockwise: Easter Bonnet Buns (p.29), Fluffy Orange
Drink (p.25), Eggy Potato Nests (p.26), Honey Shapes

baking sheets, spacing them well apart.

9. Re-mould the trimmings together and roll out again as before. Cut out 6 more shapes using the other cutter and place on the second baking sheet.

10. Cook, one sheet at a time, in the preheated oven, for 12-15 minutes until firm but only very lightly browned.

11. Leave to cool for 2 minutes and then, using a palette knife, transfer the cooked biscuits to a wire rack to cool. Cook the second batch of biscuits in the same way.

12. Now make the icing. Sift the icing sugar into a small bowl and stir in enough water to form a smooth, fairly firm icing. Put icing into a piping bag fitted with a small star nozzle. (Ask an adult to do this for you.)

13. When biscuits are cold, pipe faces on each one and 3 stars down the length of each biscuit. Leave to set for a few minutes, then lightly press a silver ball into each ice star. Leave to set completely before serving.

RAINBOW EGGS

Makes 4

INGREDIENTS	YOU WILL NEED
4 eggs (with pale shells)	medium saucepan
water, to cover	tablespoon
1 tablespoon colouring	coloured non-toxic felt-tip pens

Preparation time: 15 minutes

Cooking time: 10 minutes

1. Put the eggs into the saucepan and cover them with cold water. Carefully stir in the colouring.

2. Put the saucepan over a high heat and bring to the boil. Turn the heat down and simmer for 10 minutes.

3. Carefully remove the eggs from the pan with a tablespoon. Drain off the coloured water and re-fill the pan with cold water. Put the eggs back in the pan and leave them to cool for at least 10 minutes.

4. When they are cold, lift the eggs from the water and pat dry with kitchen paper towels. Now decorate their shells with pretty patterns or faces, using the felt-tip pens. Leave them to dry in egg cups.

5. To serve, shell the eggs and eat them with slices of brown bread and butter.

P·I·C·N·I·C·S

eddy Bears love those warm summer days that are ideal for picnics! They all help to prepare the food and pack it up carefully. Then they set off in search of the perfect place to picnic. And when every one of the sandwiches has gone, and nearly all the biscuits, they like nothing better than a peaceful snooze in the shade.

When you prepare your own picnic, remember to put the delicate foods in solid containers and wrap the sandwiches carefully. Don't forget to take the paper plates and cups, plastic knives and forks and lots of napkins. And when you go home, please remember to take the litter with you.

PITTA SALAD PARCELS

Makes 4

INGREDIENTS	YOU WILL NEED
3 eggs	medium saucepan
1 tomato	knife, for chopping
8 slices cucumber	chopping board
2 crisp lettuce leaves	plate
3 tablespoons salad cream	fork
salt and pepper to taste	tablespoon
2 pitta breads	paper napkins for serving

Preparation time: 15-20 minutes
Cooking time: 10 minutes

1. Put the eggs into a saucepan and cover them with cold water. Bring the water to the boil over a moderate heat and then leave to simmer for 10 minutes.
2. Take the pan off the heat and drain off the water. Refill the pan with cold water and leave the eggs to cool for at least 10 minutes.
3. Chop up the tomato and the cucumber into fairly small pieces and cut the lettuce into long shreds.
4. Peel the shells off the eggs and put the eggs on a plate. Mash them finely with a fork and add the salad cream and a little salt and pepper. Mix thoroughly.
5. Now stir in the chopped tomato and the cucumber.
6. Place the pitta breads on a clean surface and cut each one in half crossways. Open them up very carefully to make 4 pockets.
7. Now gently push a little shredded lettuce into the bottom of each pitta pocket. Spoon the egg mayonnaise mixture on top and level the surface with a knife.
8. To serve, wrap each one in a paper napkin.

SUPER PICNIC SPLITS

Makes 8

INGREDIENTS	YOU WILL NEED
1 teaspoon corn oil	fish slice
8 pork sausages	absorbent paper
100 g (4 oz) full fat soft cheese, softened	plate
	medium bowl
2 tablespoons cucumber or tomato relish	tablespoon
	fork
2 cocktail gherkins	chopping board
	small knife, for cutting
	teaspoon

Preparation time: 10-15 minutes
Cooling time: 20 minutes
Cooking time: 15 minutes

1. Grill the sausages under a moderate heat for 15 minutes until they are golden and cooked through.
2. Transfer the sausages to a sheet of absorbent paper on a plate, using the fish slice. Leave them to cool for 20 minutes.
3. In a medium mixing bowl, mix the cheese and the relish together with a fork until they are thoroughly combined.
4. Place the sausages on a board. Cut carefully along the length of each one, but don't cut all the way through.
5. Carefully open up the sausages and, using a teaspoon, fill each one with the cheese mixture.
6. Close up the sausages and run a fork along the length of the cheese mixture to make a pattern. Arrange a few slices of gherkin on each one.

SARDINE PUFFS

Makes 12

INGREDIENTS
1 × 120 g (4½ oz) can
  sardines in tomato sauce
25 g (1 oz) Cheddar cheese
a little flour, for
  sprinkling
1 × 368 g (13 oz) packet
  frozen puff pastry,
  thawed
a little water, to seal
a little beaten egg, to glaze
2 teaspoons sesame seeds

YOU WILL NEED
small bowl
fork
grater
rolling pin
6 cm (2½ inch) round
  biscuit cutter
5 cm (2 inch) round biscuit
  cutter
1 bun tray (for 12 buns)
teaspoon
pastry brush
wire rack

Preparation time: 25 minutes
Cooking time: 25-30 minutes

1. Heat the oven to 200°C, 400°F, Gas Mark 6. Ask an adult to help you open the can of sardines.
2. Put the sardines into a bowl and mash with a fork.
3. Grate the cheese (watch your fingers!) and add to the bowl. Mix the sardines and the cheese together well.
4. Sprinkle a clean work surface and a rolling pin with flour. Roll out the puff pastry thinly to make a 33×35 cm (13×14 inch) rectangle.
5. Using the larger cutter, cut out 12 rounds to form the bases of the Sardine Puffs. Cut them close together as you go, so that you will be able to cut out 12 lids from the same pastry.
6. Now cut out 12 rounds using the smaller cutter.

7. Press the 12 larger rounds into the hollows in the bun tray. Add a teaspoon of the sardine mixture to each one and level the surface with a spoon. Brush the smaller rounds with water on one side and place them (wet side down) on the sardine mixture. Prick the centre of the pastry lids with a fork and then press each one down firmly.
8. Brush the surfaces with beaten egg and sprinkle with sesame seeds. Cook in the preheated oven for 25-30 minutes until they are risen, golden brown and cooked through.
9. Remove the bun tray from the oven, using oven gloves.
10. Leave them to cool for a few minutes and then use a fork to lift the puffs on to a wire rack to cool.

HONEYED RICE SALAD

Serves 6

INGREDIENTS
pinch of salt
100 g (4 oz) long-grain
  white rice
100 g (4 oz) Double
  Gloucester cheese
2 spring onions
2 sticks celery
1 red apple
¼ cucumber
3 tablespoons canned
  sweetcorn
2 tablespoons sultanas
50 g (2 oz) salted peanuts (optional)

YOU WILL NEED
medium saucepan
sieve
knife, for cutting
chopping board
can opener
large bowl
tablespoon
small bowl
serving bowl

Dressing:
4 tablespoons salad cream
1-2 tablespoons clear honey
salt and pepper to taste

Preparation time: 25 minutes
Cooking time: 12-15 minutes

1. Put a medium saucepan of salted water on to boil.
When the water is boiling, add the rice and boil for
12-15 minutes until the rice is tender and cooked.
2. Ask an adult to help you drain the rice in a sieve.
Rinse the rice in cold water and then drain again.
3. Cut the cheese into small cubes. Trim and chop the
onions and the celery. Quarter the apple and remove
the core before chopping into neat pieces. Chop the
cucumber.
4. Put the cheese, chopped apple, sweetcorn, sultanas,
onions, cucumber, celery and peanuts (if you are using
them) into a large bowl. Mix them all up together with a
spoon.
5. Now make the dressing. Put the salad cream into a
small bowl with the honey and a little salt and pepper to
taste. Stir them well until combined.
6. Add the dressing to the cheese mixture and mix well
together with a spoon.
7. Stir in the rice and mix well until everything is
evenly combined.
8. To serve, spoon the salad into a bowl. It will look
pretty in a glass bowl, if you have one the right size.

CREAMY TUNA SPECIALS

Makes 4

INGREDIENTS	YOU WILL NEED
1 × 198 (7 oz) can tuna	can opener
2 spring onions	medium bowl
2 crisp lettuce leaves	knife, for cutting
10 slices cucumber	chopping board
4 tablespoons mayonnaise	tablespoon
3 tablespoons tomato	bread knife
ketchup	knife, for spreading
4 crisp round rolls	teaspoon
40 g (1½ oz) butter	paper napkins, for serving
4 slices tomato	

Preparation time: 20 minutes

1. Open the can of tuna (you may need an adult to help)
and pour off the liquid. Break the tuna into fine flakes
and put it into a bowl.
2. Trim and chop the spring onions and cut the lettuce
into shreds. Add them to the tuna in the bowl. Chop 6
slices of cucumber and add to the other ingredients.
3. Now add the mayonnaise and tomato ketchup and
mix all the ingredients up together with a spoon.
4. Put the rolls on a chopping board and carefully cut off
about a third off the top of each one. Put the tops to one
side to use as lids later.
5. Pull the soft bread out from the centre of the rolls and
butter the insides. Now butter the lids.
6. Now use a teaspoon to spoon the tuna mixture into
the hollowed-out rolls. Place a slice of cucumber and
tomato on top of each one. Arrange the lids on top. Make
sure you have some napkins to serve them with!

STICKY BANANA SLICE

Makes 10-12 slices

INGREDIENTS	YOU WILL NEED
a little oil, for greasing	pastry brush
75 g (3 oz) hard margarine, softened	900 g (2 lb) loaf tin
	greaseproof paper
175 g (6 oz) caster sugar	scissors
3 eggs	medium bowl
450 g (1 lb) bananas	wooden spoon
225 g (8 oz) self-raising flour, sifted	plate
	fork
For the glaze:	sieve
2 tablespoons icing sugar	large metal spoon
1 tablespoon clear honey	knife
1 tablespoon lemon juice	wire rack
	small saucepan
	tablespoon

Preparation time: 25 minutes
Cooking time: 1 hour 17 minutes

1. Heat the oven to 180°C, 350°F, Gas Mark 4. Brush the base and sides of a 900 g (2 lb) loaf tin with the oil. Cut a piece of greaseproof paper to fit onto the base of the tin. Put this into position and grease lightly.
2. Put the margarine and sugar into the medium bowl and mix well with a wooden spoon until light and fluffy. (You could use a food mixer, if you would rather, but always get an adult to show you how.)
3. Add the eggs one by one, beating well with a wooden spoon (or food mixer). The mixture will be really runny at this stage.
4. Peel the bananas and put them on a plate. Mash them with a fork until smooth. Add to the mixture in the bowl and stir well.
5. Sift the flour into the bowl and stir into the mixture using a large metal spoon.
6. Turn the mixture into the prepared tin and level the surface with a knife.
7. Cook in a preheated oven for 1 hour 15 minutes until well risen, golden brown and cooked through. If necessary, cover with foil to prevent overbrowning.
8. Turn the cake out of the tin onto a wire rack, using

oven gloves. Remove the greaseproof paper and turn the loaf the right way up. Leave it on the rack to cool.
9. Now you can make the glaze. Put the icing sugar, honey and lemon juice in a small saucepan and stir until melted, then bring to a boil. Boil for 2 minutes, then brush the melted mixture over the surface of the cake several times until you have used it all up.
10. Leave the cake to cool and serve out in slices.

CRUNCHY HONEY BARS

Makes 12

INGREDIENTS	YOU WILL NEED
a little oil, for greasing	pastry brush
75 g (3 oz) hard margarine	shallow 20 cm (8 inch) square baking tin
75 g (3 oz) demerara sugar	
2 tablespoons clear honey	tablespoon
75 g (3 oz) rolled porridge oats	medium saucepan
	wooden spoon
75 g (3 oz) muesli	chopping board
50 g (2 oz) self-raising flour, sifted	sieve
	round-bladed knife
25 g (1 oz) shredded coconut	

Left to right: Choc and Orange Cookies, Honeyed Rice Salad (p.34), Creamy Tuna Specials (p.35)

Preparation time: 20 minutes
Cooking time: 30-35 minutes

1. Heat the oven to 180°C, 350°F, Gas Mark 4. Brush the base and sides of a shallow baking tin with the oil.
2. Put the margarine, sugar and honey in a medium saucepan and place over a gentle heat. Stir with a wooden spoon until the ingredients have melted.
3. Remove from the heat and place the saucepan on a heatproof chopping board. Stir in the rolled oats and the muesli, and then stir in the flour. Mix them all well together until thoroughly blended. Leave to cool.
4. Press the mixture into the greased tin and level the surface with a knife. Sprinkle with the shredded coconut and pat down lightly.
5. Cook in the preheated oven for 25-30 minutes until lightly golden.
6. Remove from the oven, using oven gloves, and leave to cool for 5 minutes.
7. Mark out 12 fingers on the biscuit while it is still warm. Leave it to cool in the tin.
8. When the biscuit is cold, break it into 12 bars.

CHOC AND ORANGE COOKIES

Makes 12

INGREDIENTS	YOU WILL NEED
a little oil, for greasing	pastry brush, for greasing
100 g (4 oz) butter or hard margarine, softened	2 baking sheets
75 g (3 oz) caster sugar	large bowl
50 g (2 oz) soft light brown sugar	grater
½ teaspoon finely grated orange rind	wooden spoon
	sieve
1 egg	large metal spoon
175 g (6 oz) plain white flour, sifted	wire rack
½ teaspoon bicarbonate of soda, sifted	
100 g (4 oz) chocolate chips	

Preparation time: 25-30 minutes
Cooking time: 12-15 minutes (for each batch)

1. Heat the oven to 190°C, 375°F, Gas Mark 5. Lightly grease 2 baking sheets with oil, using a pastry brush.
2. Put the butter or margarine, caster sugar and brown sugar into a large mixing bowl. Add the orange rind and, using a wooden spoon, mix the ingredients together until soft.
3. Crack the egg into the mixture and beat well with the wooden spoon (or food mixer) until fluffy.
4. Sift the flour and bicarbonate of soda into the mixture and stir them in thoroughly, using a large metal spoon. When the mixture is evenly blended stir in the chocolate chips.
5. Divide the mixture evenly into 12 portions. Mould each portion into a ball-shape and place them, 6 at a time and spaced well apart, on each baking sheet.
6. Press each one down to form a 7.5 cm (3 inch) round.
7. Place one baking sheet of cookies in the preheated oven and cook for 12-15 minutes until lightly golden. Remove the baking sheet from the oven, using oven gloves, and put it to one side to cool.
8. Cook the second batch of cookies in the same way.
9. When all the cookies have cooled a little, transfer them from the baking sheets to a wire rack and leave them until they are quite cold.

B·A·R·B·E·C·U·E·S · & H·A·L·L·O·W·E·E·N

As lovers of the great outdoors, Teddy Bears enjoy barbecues as much as picnics. And they don't mind dressing up to scare their friends at Halloween, as long as there's something warm and comforting in the kitchen when they get home! Outdoor cooking requires special equipment, but we have come up with lots of recipes that taste just as sizzling good cooked indoors in your oven or under the grill. So even if it's raining outside you can still enjoy the barbecue flavour without missing all the fun.

BEARS' BEANFEAST

Serves 4

INGREDIENTS
1 large onion
1 teaspoon corn oil
8 chipolata sausages
1×450 g (1 lb) can baked beans
75 g (3 oz) frozen mixed
  vegetables
2 slices processed Cheddar
  cheese

YOU WILL NEED
knife, for chopping
chopping board
teaspoon
frying pan
fish slice
plate
wooden spoon
can opener
tiny cocktail cutter

Preparation time: 15 minutes
Cooking time: 25 minutes

1. Peel and chop the onion and put it to one side.
2. Put the oil into a frying pan and heat it gently. Add the sausages and cook gently for about 10 minutes, turning frequently with a fish slice until the sausages are golden brown all over.
3. Transfer the sausages to a plate with the fish slice. Fry the chopped onion in the frying pan for 5 minutes, stirring often with the wooden spoon.
4. Carefully drain off the oil from the pan. Add the baked beans and frozen mixed vegetables and stir well.
5. Cook until the mixture is bubbling, then return the sausages to the pan and cook gently for 6 minutes, stirring occasionally.
6. Cut out small shapes from the cheese, using the tiny cutter, and arrange these on top of the mixture. Serve hot with chunks of crusty bread.

CHEESY BAKED POTATOES

Serves 4

INGREDIENTS
4 medium potatoes
salt and pepper to taste
25 g (1 oz) soft margarine
10 slices processed
  Cheddar cheese
a little pickle

YOU WILL NEED
medium saucepan
colander
chopping board
sharp knife
pastry brush
foil, for wrapping
knife and fork
spoon

Preparation time: 15 minutes
Cooking time: 55 minutes
Cooling time: 10 minutes

1. Heat the oven to 200°F, 400°F, Gas Mark 6.
2. Wash the potatoes in cold water until they are quite clean, but do not peel them.
3. Put the potatoes into a saucepan and cover them with cold water. Bring the water to the boil and boil the potatoes for 15 minutes.
4. Drain the potatoes in a colander (ask an adult to help you). Leave to cool for 10 minutes.
5. Put the cool potatoes on a board and, using a sharp knife, cut each one into equal slices.
6. Sprinkle the potato slices with salt and pepper to taste. Now press the potato slices gently back into shape to form 4 whole potatoes.
7. Melt the margarine in a saucepan and brush it over the potatoes with the pastry brush.
8. Wrap potatoes individually in pieces of foil, to cover each one completely. Cook in the preheated oven for 40 minutes until they feel soft when squeezed gently. Make sure you wear oven gloves to test them.
9. Remove the potatoes from the oven and carefully turn back the foil to expose them. Using a knife and fork, separate the potato slices to open slightly.
10. Put half a cheese slice and, if you like, a little of your favourite pickle in between each slice of potato.
11. Press the potatoes back into shape and serve hot.

BARBECUED BABY CORN

Serves 4

INGREDIENTS	YOU WILL NEED
2 tablespoons tomato or	tablespoon
mild chilli relish	small saucepan
1 tablespoon clear honey	wooden spoon
50 g (2 oz) butter	baking sheet
16 baby corn cobs	fork
4 crumpets

Preparation time: 10 minutes

Cooking time: 15 minutes

1. Heat the oven to 190°C, 375°F, Gas Mark 5.
2. Put the relish, honey and 25 g (1 oz) of the butter into a small saucepan and heat gently until they have melted. Stir occasionally with the wooden spoon.
3. Add the corn cobs to the saucepan and stir until they are well coated with the mixture.
4. Using the spoon, lift the corn cobs out and arrange them on a baking sheet. Cook in a preheated oven for 15 minutes until cooked through and lightly golden.
5. Meanwhile, toast the crumpets and spread with the remaining butter. Keep warm.
6. Using oven gloves to protect your hands, remove the sheet of corn cobs from the oven. Using a fork, lift 4 cobs onto each warm, buttered crumpet. Serve hot.

CRISPY HONEY DRUMSTICKS

Serves 4

INGREDIENTS	YOU WILL NEED
a little oil, for greasing	pastry brush
25 g (1 oz) Cheddar cheese	baking sheet
2 tablespoons tomato	grater
ketchup	2 plates
4 teaspoons clear honey	tablespoon
1 × 28 g packet salted	small bowl
crisps	fish slice
4 chicken drumsticks	paper napkins

Preparation time: 10 minutes

Cooking time: 30 minutes

1. Heat the oven to 190°C, 375°F, Gas Mark 5. Brush the baking sheet with the oil.
2. Grate the cheese and put it to one side on a plate.
3. Put the tomato ketchup and the honey into a small bowl and mix well together.
4. Crush the crisps in the bag and empty them onto a plate. Add the grated cheese and mix well.
5. Using the pastry brush, coat the drumsticks thickly with the tomato mixture. Roll the drumsticks in the crushed crisps and cheese until they are evenly coated. You can use your hands to make sure the mixture sticks on properly.
6. Place the drumsticks on the greased baking sheet and cook in the preheated oven for about 30 minutes until the drumsticks are cooked through.

7. Using oven gloves to protect your hands, remove the baking sheet from the oven and leave the drumsticks to cool for 3 minutes.

8. Using a fish slice, gently lift the drumsticks from the baking sheet. Serve with paper napkins.

TRICKY TOAST TREATS

Serves 4 (makes 8)

INGREDIENTS	YOU WILL NEED
1 banana	knife, for cutting
25 g (1 oz) soft margarine	chopping board
¼ teaspoon ground cinnamon	teaspoon
	small bowl
25 g (1 oz) soft light brown sugar	fork
	bread knife
4 slices fruited malt loaf, about 5 mm (¼ inch) thick	bread board
	knife, for spreading
	8 cocktail or satay sticks

Preparation time: 10-15 minutes
Cooking time: 3-4 minutes

1. Peel the banana and cut it into chunky slices.
2. Put the margarine, cinnamon and sugar into a small bowl and mix well together with a fork until soft and combined.
3. Toast the slices of malt loaf on both sides.
4. Place toasted malt loaf on a board and spread each slice on one side only with the cinnamon mixture.
6. Cut each slice into quarters. Thread a piece of bread onto a cocktail stick, then a banana slice, then another piece of bread and finally another slice of banana. Repeat this to make 8 Tricky Toast Treats altogether.

CRUNCHY MARSHMALLOW MELTS

Serves 4

INGREDIENTS	YOU WILL NEED
8 marshmallows (a mixture of pink and white)	scissors
	foil
	baking sheet
8 digestive biscuits	

Preparation time: 10 minutes
Cooking time: 10 minutes

1. Preheat the oven to 180°C, 350°F, Gas Mark 4.
2. Snip the marshmallows into quarters.
3. Place 4 biscuits flat on a work surface. Cover each one with 8 marshmallow quarters. Place the remaining biscuits on top to form 4 sandwiches.
4. Wrap each sandwich individually in foil to cover them completely. Place on a baking sheet.
5. Cook in a preheated oven for 10 minutes or until the marshmallows have melted.
6. Using oven gloves to protect your hands, remove the baking sheet from the oven. Leave to cool for 2 minutes, then very carefully remove the foil and leave the Marshmallow Melts to cool before serving.

Top left: Cheesy Baked Potatoes (p.39); Top Right: Tricky Toast Treats; Bottom left: Crispy Honey Drumsticks; Bottom Right: Iced Spice Biscuits (p.42)

MIDNIGHT MOUSSE

Serves 4

INGREDIENTS
100 g (4 oz) plain chocolate
  chips
2 eggs
1 tablespoon icing sugar,
  sifted
¼ teaspoon vanilla
  essence
150 ml (¼ pint) double
  cream

YOU WILL NEED
medium heatproof bowl
medium saucepan
3 bowls
wooden spoon
tablespoon
teaspoon
rotary hand whisk
4 individual serving
  glasses

Preparation time: 20-25 minutes
Cooking time: about 5 minutes
Setting time: 2 hours

1. Put the chocolate chips into a medium heatproof bowl and place the bowl over a medium saucepan filled with hot, not boiling, water. Place over a low heat until the chocolate chips have melted. Remove the bowl from the pan, using oven gloves. Turn off the heat.
2. Ask an adult to separate the eggs for you. Add the egg yolks to the chocolate mixture and put the egg whites into a separate bowl.
3. Add the icing sugar and the vanilla essence to the chocolate and the egg yolks and mix together.
4. Whisk the egg whites in a bowl using a rotary hand whisk, until they stand in stiff peaks. Whisk the cream in another bowl until soft peaks form.

5. Gently stir the cream into the chocolate mixture with a large metal spoon. Add the egg whites, a little at a time and very gently fold and stir them into the mixture until they are evenly combined. Ask an adult to show you how.
6. Pour the mixture into 4 glasses and leave to set in the refrigerator for at least 2 hours, or overnight.

ICED SPICE COOKIES

Makes 18

INGREDIENTS
a little oil, for greasing
175 g (6 oz) plain white
  flour, sifted
1 teaspoon ground
  cinnamon, sifted
50 g (2 oz) caster sugar
100 g (4 oz) butter or hard
  margarine, softened
a little flour, for
  sprinkling
Icing:
225 g (8 oz) icing, sugar,
  sifted
6-7 teaspoons warm water
To decorate:
6 glacé cherries, halved
18 jelly tots or smarties
6 walnut halves
2 teaspoons hundreds and
  thousands

YOU WILL NEED
pastry brush
baking sheet
sieve
teaspoon
large bowl
rolling pin
6 cm (2½ inch) round
  fluted biscuit cutter
palette knife
wire rack
medium bowl
wooden spoon

Preparation time: 25 minutes
Cooling time: 20 minutes
Cooking time: 25 minutes

1. Heat the oven to 160°C, 325°F, Gas Mark 3. Lightly brush the baking sheet with oil.
2. Sift the flour and cinnamon into a large bowl. Stir in the sugar. Add the butter and rub it in with your fingertips until the mixture begins to form a dough. Knead it well in the bowl until you have a smooth ball.
3. Sprinkle the work surface and rolling pin with the flour. Roll out the mixture to 5 mm (¼ inch) thickness.
4. Cut out about 17 rounds, using the fluted biscuit cutter. Carefully lift these rounds onto the greased baking sheet, using the palette knife.
5. Re-knead and re-roll the trimmings and cut out more biscuits, to make 24 rounds in all.
6. Cook in the preheated oven for 25 minutes, or until the biscuits are just lightly golden.
7. Using oven gloves, remove the baking sheet from the oven. Leave the biscuits to cool for 5 minutes.
8. Transfer the biscuits to a wire rack and leave them to cool for a further 15 minutes.
9. Now you can make the icing. Sift the icing sugar into a medium bowl. Add the warm water and mix well with a wooden spoon until smooth.
10. Using a teaspoon, spread the icing over the surface of each biscuit and leave to set for 2 minutes.
11. Decorate 6 biscuits with the cherries, 6 with jelly tots or smarties, 6 with the walnut halves and 6 with hundreds and thousands. Leave to set before serving.

MINTED HOT CHOCOLATE

Serves 4

INGREDIENTS	YOU WILL NEED
600 ml (1 pint) milk	medium saucepan
75 g (3 oz) chocolate-covered peppermint creams	board
	knife
2 tablespoons drinking chocolate	tablespoon
	wooden spoon
To finish:	small bowl
4 tablespoons whipping cream	rotary hand whisk
a little drinking chocolate, for sprinkling	spoon
	4 small mugs

Preparation time: 10 minutes
Cooking time: 3 minutes

1. Put the milk into a medium saucepan and heat until hot, but not boiling.
2. Remove the saucepan from the heat and place on a board. Cut the peppermint creams into small pieces. Add them to the milk, together with the drinking chocolate and stir well until melted and smooth.
3. Put the cream into a small bowl and whisk until soft peaks form.
4. Pour the milky mixture into 4 mugs and top each one with a spoonful of whipped cream and then sprinkle with a little drinking chocolate.

P·R·E·S·E·N·T·S

One thing all Teddy Bears like doing is giving presents on those special days: birthdays, Christmas Day, Mother's Day, Father's Day, and of course, Valentine's Day! What could be better than a homemade gift that is truly decorative to look at and tastes simply delicious. Meringue Mushrooms, Little Pink Mice and Fairy Mint Creams make perfect presents. Pretty packaging need not be too expensive, either. We have given you some ideas – lots of small containers look really special when you tie a ribbon around them.

LITTLE PINK MICE

Makes 10

INGREDIENTS
1 sheet rice paper
2 egg whites
175 g (6 oz) granulated sugar
200 g (7 oz) desiccated
  coconut
¼ teaspoon red food colouring
To decorate:
1 glacé cherry
20 silver balls
20 flaked almonds
10×7.5 cm (3 inch) lengths
  of red liquorice lace

YOU WILL NEED
baking sheet
large bowl
rotary hand whisk
teaspoon
fork
board
knife
wire rack
scissors
cocktail stick
a pretty shallow basket
  or silver board

Preparation time: 25 minutes
Cooking time: 45 minutes

1. Heat the oven to 140°C, 275°F, Gas Mark 1. Place the piece of rice paper on a baking sheet.
2. Ask an adult to separate the eggs. Put the egg whites into a large bowl and whisk them with a rotary hand whisk until they are really stiff and fluffy.
3. Add the sugar, coconut and red food colouring and mix with a fork until evenly blended and coloured.
4. Divide the mixture into 10 equal parts. Make each portion into a round shape. Place them all on a board and give each one a tapering point at one end to make a mouse's nose.
5. Lift onto the rice paper on the baking sheet. Cut the glacé cherry into 10 small pieces and put a small piece on each tapering point to form a nose. Add 2 silver balls to each one as eyes and then push 2 flaked almonds into each one for the ears.
6. Cook at the bottom of a preheated oven for 45 minutes until pale in colour.
7. Using oven gloves to protect your hands, remove the baking sheet of mice from the oven. Leave to cool for 15 minutes.
8. Lift the mice and rice paper onto a wire rack to cool completely. When cold, trim the rice paper round each mouse, using scissors to neaten.

9. Make a small hole at the tail end of each mouse with a cocktail stick and insert a length of liquorice lace.
10. To pack as a present, either arrange the mice in a pretty shallow basket or on a silver cake board.

SNAP AND CRACKLE CAKES

Makes 9

INGREDIENTS
200 g (7 oz) packet plain
  chocolate cake covering
50 g (2 oz) chopped nuts
50 g (2 oz) sultanas
40 g (1½ oz) bran flakes,
  coarsely crushed
finely grated rind of
  1 orange
To decorate:
9 glacé cherry halves

YOU WILL NEED
medium heatproof bowl
medium saucepan
cloth
grater
wooden spoon
9 paper bun cases
1 bun tray
pretty tin
ribbon

Preparation time: 20 minutes
Cooking time: 5-6 minutes

1. Break the cake covering into small pieces in a heatproof bowl. (You may need an adult to help you.)
2. Place the bowl over a saucepan of hot, not boiling, water. Leave the chocolate to melt.
3. Using your oven gloves, remove the bowl from the saucepan and place it on a cloth on the work surface.
4. Add the chopped nuts, sultanas, bran flakes and orange rind and mix everything together well with a wooden spoon.
5. Using a teaspoon, spoon the mixture into the 9 paper bun cases in the bun tray and decorate each one with a halved glacé cherry. Leave to set for 1 hour.

MERINGUE MUSHROOMS

Makes 12

INGREDIENTS
2 egg whites
100 g (4 oz) caster sugar
a few drops red food
 colouring
silver balls
3 tablespoons raspberry
 jam

YOU WILL NEED
baking sheet
a sheet of non-stick
 silicone paper
medium bowl
rotary hand whisk
tablespoon
piping bag
1 cm (½ inch) plain nozzle
tweezers
wire rack
small sharp knife
paper plates
plastic wrap
pretty ribbon

Preparation time: 25 minutes

Cooking time: 3-4 hours

1. Heat the oven to 110°C, 225°F, Gas Mark ¼. Line a baking sheet with a sheet of non-stick silicone paper.
2. Ask an adult to separate the eggs. Put the whites into a medium bowl. Using a rotary hand whisk or food mixer, whisk the egg whites until they are stiff.
3. Sprinkle over 50 g (2 oz) of the sugar, add a few drops of red food colouring and whisk again until stiff and glossy.
4. Using a tablespoon, lightly fold in the remaining sugar. Put the mixture into a large pastry bag fitted with a 1 cm (½ inch) nozzle (ask an adult to help).
5. Pipe 12 mounds of meringue, each measuring about 5 cm (2 inches) across, onto the baking sheet. These will be the mushroom tops. Pipe the remaining mixture to make the stalks. These should be smaller, about 2 cm (¾ inch) across, with a sharply pointed top.
6. Using clean tweezers, stick about 5 silver balls lightly onto each of the larger meringue mounds.
7. Cook the meringues in the preheated oven for 3-4 hours until set and completely dried out.
8. When the meringues are ready, remove the baking sheet from the oven, using oven gloves. Transfer them to a wire rack to cool for 15 minutes. (These can now be stored in an airtight tin until they are required.)
9. To serve: with a small pointed knife, scrape a small hole in the base of each of the larger meringues. Now dip the pointed ends of the smaller meringues into the jam and insert into the hole of the larger ones.
10. To pack the meringues as a present, put them on 2 paper plates wrapped in plastic wrap and tie a pretty ribbon around. Eat them within a few hours.

Left: Little Pink Mice (p.45); Right: Fairy Mint Creams

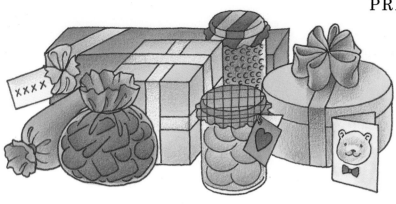

CHOC-DIPPED MALLOWS

Makes 18

INGREDIENTS
100g (4 oz) plain or milk
  chocolate chips
2 tablespoons hundreds
  and thousands
2 tablespoons chopped
  mixed nuts
2 tablespoons chocolate
  strands
18 marshmallows (pink
  and white)

YOU WILL NEED
baking sheet
sheet of greaseproof paper
medium heatproof bowl
medium saucepan
tablespoon
3 small plates
18 cocktail sticks
cloth
spoon
To serve: 1 grapefruit

Preparation time: 25 minutes
Cooking time: 3-4 minutes

1. Line a baking sheet with greaseproof paper.
2. Put the chocolate chips into a heatproof bowl and place over a medium saucepan of hot, not boiling, water, over a low heat. Leave the chocolate to melt.
3. Put the hundreds and thousands, chopped nuts and the chocolate strands onto 3 separate plates.
4. Push a cocktail stick firmly into each marshmallow. Using oven gloves, transfer the saucepan and bowl of chocolate from the heat to a cloth on the work surface.
5. Holding the cocktail sticks firmly, dip about half of each marshmallow into the chocolate, then into the hundreds and thousands, nuts or chocolate strands.
6. Place the dipped marshmallows on the prepared baking sheet and leave them to set for at least 1 hour.
7. To give the Choc-Dipped Mallows as a present, push the cocktail sticks into 2 grapefruit halves.

FAIRY MINT CREAMS

Makes about 45-50

INGREDIENTS
1 egg white
a few drops oil of
  peppermint or
  peppermint essence
a few drops green food
  colouring (optional)
350 g (12 oz) icing sugar,
  sifted
a little extra icing sugar,
  for sprinkling
To decorate:
silver balls and tiny
  sweets

YOU WILL NEED
baking sheet
sheet of greaseproof paper
medium bowl
fork
sieve
wooden spoon
rolling pin
tiny biscuit/cocktail
  cutters
glass storage jar
ribbon

Preparation time: 25-30 minutes

1. Line a baking sheet with the greaseproof paper and put to one side.
2. Ask an adult to separate the egg. Put the egg white, peppermint essence and food colouring into a medium bowl. Beat together with a fork until just frothy and broken up.
3. Add half the quantity of icing sugar and mix well with a wooden spoon.
4. Stir in more icing sugar and start mixing by hand. Add the remaining sugar and continue mixing until it is all gathered together. Mould the mixture well by hand until smooth and free from cracks.
5. Sprinkle the work surface and rolling pin with icing sugar. Roll out the mixture to 5 mm (¼ inch) thickness.
6. Using tiny biscuit/cocktail cutters, cut out as many shapes as possible and place them on the prepared baking sheet.
7. Re-knead and re-roll the trimmings to make between 45 and 50 shapes altogether.
8. Decorate the shapes with silver balls and tiny sweets, pressing them in firmly to stick. Leave them to set for at least 4 hours, or overnight.
9. To give the Fairy Mint Creams as a present, pack them in a glass storage jar, tied with a ribbon.

C·H·R·I·S·T·M·A·S

Christmas comes but once a year, and when it does it brings good cheer . . . and lots of surprises! Around Christmas most Teddy Bears prefer to stay indoors, keeping warm and cosy, avoiding any unnecessary exertion, and indulging in one or two seasonal favourites from the kitchen – Bumper Christmas Burgers and Starry-Eyed Mincepies, for instance. They like making their own Christmas Decoration Cookies to hang on the tree on Christmas Day, so why not join them?

FINGER-DIPPING TURKEY BITES

Serves 4

INGREDIENTS	YOU WILL NEED
350g (12 oz) cooked turkey meat	sharp knife
2 eggs	chopping board
100 g (4 oz) fresh breadcrumbs	fork
	shallow dish
50 g (2 oz) sage and onion stuffing mix	medium bowl
	tablespoon
1 tablespoon grated Parmesan cheese (optional)	frying pan
	fish slice
	plate
3 tablespoons corn oil	

To serve:
a selection of dips, relishes and mayonnaise

Preparation time: 20 minutes
Cooking time: 4-5 minutes

1. Cut the turkey meat into bite-sized pieces.
2. Beat the eggs and put to one side in a shallow dish.
3. Put the breadcrumbs and stuffing mix into a bowl. Add the cheese, if you are using it, and mix well.
4. Dip the pieces of turkey into the beaten egg and then coat them all over in breadcrumbs and stuffing.
5. Heat the oil in a large frying pan and fry the turkey bites (half at a time) for about 4-5 minutes until they are golden brown, turning occasionally with a fish slice. (Ask an adult to help you.)
6. Lift the Turkey Bites from the frying pan, using a fish slice, and place them on a sheet of absorbent paper on a plate. Cook the rest of the turkey in the same way.
7. Serve the Turkey Bites, warm or cold, with tasty dips.

BUMPER CHRISTMAS BURGERS

Makes 4

INGREDIENTS	YOU WILL NEED
1 small onion	chopping board
175 g (6 oz) cooked turkey meat	knife, for chopping
	large bowl
225 g (8 oz) pork sausagemeat	teaspoon
	tablespoon

a good pinch of dried mixed herbs	large frying pan
	fish slice
½ teaspoon salt	
pepper to taste	
a little flour, for dusting	
1 tablespoon corn oil, for frying	

To serve:
4 sesame seed baps
4 crisp lettuce leaves
4 slices processed Cheddar cheese
8 slices tomato

Preparation time: 20 minutes
Cooking time: 10 minutes

1. Peel and chop the onion finely. Ask an adult to help you to mince the turkey meat, or chop it very finely.
2. Put the sausagemeat and minced turkey into a large bowl. Add the onion, herbs and salt and pepper to taste. Mix well together by hand.
3. Lightly dust a work surface with flour. Divide the mixture into 4 portions. With lightly floured hands, mould each portion into a burger shape, about 10 cm (4 inches) in diameter.
4. Heat the oil gently in a large frying pan. Add the burgers and fry over a medium heat for about 10 minutes, turning them occasionally with a fish slice.
5. Split the sesame baps in half and place a crisp lettuce leaf on the bottom half of each one. Arrange the burgers on top of this and cover each one with a slice of cheese. Add slices of tomato to each one. Cover with the tops.

CHEESE AND RAISIN MUFFINS

Makes 12

INGREDIENTS
50 g (2 oz) Cheddar cheese
1 egg
200 g (7 oz) self-raising
  flour, sifted
1 teaspoon baking powder
good pinch of salt
50 g (2 oz) raisins or
  sultanas
25 g (1 oz) butter
150 ml (¼ pt) milk
To serve:
curd cheese, for spreading

YOU WILL NEED
bun tray (for 12 buns)
12 paper bun cases
grater
plate
small bowl
fork
sieve
large bowl
teaspoon
saucepan
wooden spoon
dessertspoon

Preparation time: 20 minutes
Cooking time: 25-30 minutes

1. Heat the oven to 180°C, 350°F, Gas Mark 4. Line a bun tray with 12 paper bun cases.
2. Grate the cheese. Beat the egg and set to one side.
3. Put the flour, baking powder, salt, raisins (or sultanas) and cheese into a large bowl and mix them together.
4. Melt the butter in a saucepan over a low heat. Remove from heat.
5. Add the beaten egg, milk and melted butter to the bowl and mix together lightly with a wooden spoon.
6. Spoon heaped dessertspoonfuls of the mixture into the 12 paper bun cases.
7. Cook in the preheated oven for 25-30 minutes until the muffins are golden brown and cooked through.
8. Using oven gloves to protect your hands, remove the bun trays from the oven. Leave the muffins to cool before cutting in half and spreading with curd cheese.

Top: Honey Ice Cream; Left: Finger-dipping Turkey Bites (p.49);
Right: Bumper Christmas Burgers (p.49)

APPLE SHORTCAKE PIE

Serves 8

INGREDIENTS
225 g (8 oz) plain flour
50 g (2 oz) caster sugar
175 g (6 oz) butter or hard
  margarine
Filling:
3 medium cooking apples
175 g (6 oz) golden syrup
50 g (2 oz) fresh white
  breadcrumbs

YOU WILL NEED
2 medium bowls
knife
rolling pin
23 cm (9 inch) ceramic flan
  dish
apple corer
potato peeler
chopping board
grater
baking sheet
tablespoon

Preparation time: 25 minutes
Cooking time: 45 minutes

1. Heat the oven to 180°C, 350°F, Gas Mark 4.
2. Put the flour in a medium bowl and add the sugar. Cut the butter into small pieces and rub it into the flour until it resembles breadcrumbs. Mould into a ball.
3. Cut about a third of the mixture off and put it to one side. Roll out the larger portion, using a rolling pin, to make a 25 cm (10 inch) round. Use the rolling pin to help lift the shortbread over the flan dish. (Don't worry if it breaks up.)
4. Press the mixture over the base and up the sides of the flan dish and trim the top edge with a knife.
5. To make the filling, peel and core the apples, then grate them. Put the golden syrup, breadcrumbs and grated apples into a bowl and mix well together.
6. Spoon the filling into the dish and smooth the surface.
7. Grate the rest of the shortbread mixture over the top of the apple filling. Press it down lightly with your fingertips. Place the dish on a baking sheet.
8. Cook in the preheated oven for 45 minutes until cooked through and lightly golden. Cover the surface with a sheet of foil during cooking, if necessary, to prevent overbrowning.
9. Using oven gloves, remove the baking sheet and dish from the oven. Leave to cool for 10 minutes before serving.

HONEY ICE CREAM

Serves 4-6

INGREDIENTS
300 ml (½ pint) double cream
6 tablespoons clear honey
150 ml (¼ pint) plain yoghurt
1 egg
chocolate drops, to
  decorate

YOU WILL NEED
2 medium bowls
rotary hand whisk
fork
tablespoon
900 g (2 lb) loaf tin

Preparation time: 20 minutes, plus freezing

1. Put the cream into a medium bowl and, using a rotary hand whisk, whisk it until soft peaks form.
2. Add the honey and yoghurt and whisk once again until the mixture is smooth and evenly combined.
3. Ask an adult to separate the egg yolk from the white for you. Add the egg yolk to the bowl of mixture. Put the egg white in another bowl and keep for later. Whisk the egg yolk into the creamy mixture.
4. Turn the mixture into a 900 g (2 lb) loaf tin and freeze for about 1 hour until the mixture is beginning to set around the edges.
5. Spoon the ice cream into a bowl and break it up finely with a fork. Whisk the egg white in another bowl until stiff. Add the egg white to the ice cream and whisk together until well combined.
6. Return the mixture to the loaf tin and freeze again for at least 4 hours before serving. Decorate with chocolate drops.

■ CHRISTMAS DECORATION COOKIES ■

Makes 20

INGREDIENTS
a little oil, for greasing
50 g (2 oz) hard margarine,
  softened
50 g (2 oz) caster sugar
1 egg
a few drops vanilla
  essence
100 g (4 oz) plain flour,
  sifted
a little extra flour, for
  sprinkling
Glaze:
1 egg yolk
¼ teaspoon red food
  colouring
¼ teaspoon green food
  colouring
To decorate:
about 1 tablespoon tiny
  sweets
silver balls
fine gold thread

YOU WILL NEED
pastry brush
baking sheet
medium bowl
wooden spoon
small bowl
fork
tablespoon
sieve
rolling pin
star biscuit cutter
palette knife
2 saucers
cocktail stick
wire rack

Preparation time: 30 minutes
Cooking time: 10-12 minutes

1. Heat the oven to 180°C, 350°F, Gas Mark 4.
With the pastry brush, lightly grease a baking
sheet with the oil.
2. Put the margarine into a medium bowl
and mix well with a wooden spoon until it
is soft. Add the sugar and beat it in well
until you have a pale, fluffy mixture.
3. Beat the egg. Add only half of it to
the mixture. Add the vanilla
essence and mix well.

4. Add the sifted flour and stir it in well until the ingredients are thoroughly combined. Mould the mixture into a smooth ball.

5. Sprinkle a little flour over the work surface and the rolling pin. Roll out the mixture to thickness of about 5 mm (¼ inch).

6. Using a star-shaped biscuit cutter, cut out about 12 shapes. Lift these carefully onto the greased baking sheet, using a palette knife.

7. Re-knead and re-roll the trimmings and cut out more shapes, to make about 20 stars altogether.

8. Now make your glaze. Stir the egg yolk until smooth. Place half the egg yolk on one of the saucers and the remaining half on another saucer. Add a few drops of red food colouring to one saucer and a few drops of green colouring to the other. Mix each one until evenly coloured.

9. Using a pastry brush, brush 10 of the cookies with red colouring and the remaining 10 cookies with green colouring. To make sure you use up each of the glazes, brush the cookies several times.

10. Sprinkle the centre of each cookie with tiny sweets and decorate each star point with a silver ball.

11. Using a cocktail stick, make a small hole in the centre of one star point on each cookie. (This will be used for threading the cookies later.)

12. Cook the cookies in the preheated oven for 10-12 minutes until they are cooked through and only very lightly browned.

13. Using oven gloves, remove the baking sheet from the oven. Leave the cookies to cool for 5 minutes, then very carefully push a cocktail stick through the little holes to open them up again.

14. Lift the cookies onto a wire rack to cool. When they are cold, thread each one with a little gold thread and tie them onto the Christmas Tree.

FROSTED GINGERBREAD TREES

Makes 8

INGREDIENTS	YOU WILL NEED
a little oil, for greasing	pastry brush
225 g (8 oz) plain flour	33×23 cm (13×9
1 teaspoon ground mixed spice	inch) Swiss roll tin
1 teaspoon ground ginger	large sheet
1 teaspoon bicarbonate of soda	greaseproof paper
75 g (3 oz) golden syrup	scissors
75 g (3 oz) black treacle	sieve
75 g (3 oz) hard margarine	teaspoon
75 g (3 oz) soft light brown sugar	large bowl
2 eggs	saucepan
200 ml (7 fl oz) milk	wooden spoon
Icing:	Christmas Tree
1 egg	biscuit cutter
100 g (4 oz) icing sugar, sifted	small bowl
To decorate:	tablespoon
small jelly sweets	knife

Preparation time: 35 minutes
Cooking time: 35 minutes

1. Heat the oven to 160°C, 325°F, Gas Mark 3. Using the pastry brush, lightly grease the base and sides of the Swiss roll tin with the oil. Line the tin with a sheet of greaseproof paper, cutting the corners to fit neatly. (Ask a grown up to show you how do to this.)
2. Sift the flour, mixed spice, ginger and bicarbonate of soda into a large bowl.
3. Put the golden syrup, black treacle, margarine and brown sugar into a saucepan and heat gently until they have melted. Remove the pan from the heat.
4. Beat 2 eggs. Add the eggs, milk and the melted mixture to the flour mixture in the bowl and mix really well together, using a wooden spoon.
5. Pour the mixture into the prepared tin and cook in the preheated oven for 30 minutes until risen and firm to the touch.
6. Using oven gloves to protect your hands, remove the tin from the oven and leave the cake to cool in the tin.
7. Turn the tin upside down on to a work surface and remove the lining paper.
8. Using a Christmas Tree cutter, cut out as many shapes as you can, pressing the cutter firmly down each time. (Keep the cake trimmings to eat, or to make a trifle.)
9. Turn the Gingerbread Trees, so they are the right way up. To make the icing, ask an adult to separate an egg for you. Lightly beat the white (you do not need the yolk) and put 2 tablespoons of it into a small bowl with the sifted icing sugar. Mix well with a wooden spoon to form a smooth, thick icing.
10. Using a knife, place a little icing on the edges of trees, to form snowy peaks. Decorate with small jelly sweets and leave to set before serving.

PINK LEMONADE

Serves 4

INGREDIENTS	YOU WILL NEED
2 large lemons	potato peeler
175 g (6 oz) granulated	medium saucepan
sugar	lemon squeezer
750 ml (1¼ pints) water	tablespoon
2 teaspoons blackcurrant	teaspoon
syrup	sieve
	jug

Preparation time: 10 minutes, plus cooling
Cooking time: 5 minutes
Cooling time: 30 minutes

1. Using a potato peeler, very thinly peel off the rinds from the lemons, taking care not to include the white part of the rind.
2. Put the lemon peelings into a saucepan with the sugar and water. Squeeze out the juice from lemons, using a lemon squeezer. Add the juice to the saucepan and stir well.
3. Bring the mixture to the boil, stirring to dissolve the sugar. Remove it from the heat and leave it to cool.
4. Strain the mixture into a jug. Add the blackcurrant syrup and stir it until it is evenly coloured. For a cool drink, serve chilled or with ice cubes.

STARRY-EYED MINCEPIES

Makes 12

INGREDIENTS	YOU WILL NEED
a little flour, for sprinkling	a bun or tartlet tin (for 12 buns/tarts)
1 × 368 g (13 oz) packet frozen shortcrust pastry, thawed	rolling pin
	7.5 cm (3 inch) round fluted cutter
1 × 450 g (1 lb) jar mincemeat	6 cm (2½ inch) round fluted cutter
a little beaten egg, to glaze	teaspoon
2 teaspoons granulated sugar, for sprinkling	pastry brush
	tiny cocktail cutter
	wire rack

Preparation time: 25 minutes
Cooking time: 20 minutes

1. Heat the oven to 190°C, 375°F, Gas Mark 5. Have ready a bun or tartlet tin (for 12 buns/tarts).
2. Sprinkle the work surface and the rolling pin with a little flour. Roll out the pastry until it is about 3 mm (⅛ inch) thick.
3. Using a 7.5 cm (3 inch) round fluted cutter, cut out 12 rounds, pressing the cutter down firmly each time. Gently press these rounds into the bun/tartlet tins.
4. Put a teaspoonful of mincemeat into each one.
5. Re-knead and re-roll the pastry trimmings and cut out 12 more rounds (for lids), using a 6 cm (2½ inch) round fluted cutter. Now, using a tiny star-shaped cutter, cut out the centres, and reserve for later.
6. Brush the underside of the lids lightly with water and place on top of mincemeat. Press down lightly.
7. Brush the pastry tops with beaten egg to glaze and arrange a tiny star on the side of each mincepie. Brush them with egg. Sprinkle the mincepies with sugar.
8. Cook in the preheated oven for 20 minutes until golden brown and cooked through.
9. Using oven gloves to protect your hands, remove the tin of mincepies from the oven. Leave the mincepies to cool in the tins for 5 minutes.

Top: Pink Lemonade; Left: Christmas Decoration Cookies (p.52); Right: Starry-eyed Mincepies; Bottom: Frosted Gingerbread Trees

F·U·N · F·O·O·D

Nobody knows better than Teddy Bears that cooking should never be boring. And sometimes they simply feel like messing around in the kitchen, without the bother of switching on ovens and grills and waiting for things to bake. They know you can make some delicious goodies, without cooking at all! That's why we've included these special recipes, which hardly involve any cooking and which are just right for those long afternoons when you don't quite know what to do. So, entertain yourself in the kitchen, and then entertain your friends and family with some of these tasty snacks.

STRIPED DOUBLE DECKERS

Serves 4

INGREDIENTS	YOU WILL NEED
1 egg	small saucepan
4 slices brown bread, ready-cut	knife, for spreading
40 g (1½ oz) margarine	2 tablespoons
2 slices white bread, ready-cut	chopping board
50 g (2 oz) soft liver pâté	fork
8 thin slices cucumber	sharp knife
1 tablespoon mayonnaise	
salt and pepper to taste	
a little mustard and cress	
To garnish: mustard and cress	

Preparation time: 25 minutes
Cooking time: 10 minutes
Cooling time: 10 minutes

1. Put the egg in the small saucepan and cover with cold water. Bring to the boil and simmer for about 10 minutes. Remove the pan from the heat, drain and refill with cold water. Leave to cool for 10 minutes.
2. Spread the brown slices of bread on one side only with the margarine. Spread the slices of white bread on both sides with the margarine.
3. Put a slice of brown bread on a board, buttered side upwards. Spread this with half the soft liver pâté and cover with 4 slices of cucumber.
4. Place a buttered slice of white bread on top.
5. When the egg is cold, peel it and mash it with the mayonnaise until you have a smooth mixture. Season with salt and pepper and mix well.
6. Spread half the egg mixture over the white bread and sprinkle with mustard and cress.
7. Place a brown slice of bread, buttered side down this time, on top and press the sandwich down.
8. Make another sandwich in the same way.
9. Using a sharp knife, cut off the crusts. Now cut each sandwich into 4 equal strips.
10. Arrange on a serving plate with mustard and cress.

SAILING BOAT SNACKS

Makes 8

INGREDIENTS	YOU WILL NEED
8 chipolata sausages	fish slice
4 stalks celery	plate
50 g (2 oz) soft cream cheese	small sharp knife
2 slices processed cheese	8 cocktail sticks
a little shredded lettuce	serving plates

Preparation time: 20 minutes
Cooking time: 15 minutes

1. Turn on the grill to a moderate heat and grill the sausages for about 15 minutes, turning them frequently. When they are brown and cooked through, remove them with a fish slice and leave them to cool.
2. Meanwhile, trim the celery stalks and cut them into lengths of about 10 cm (4 inches). Cut off a very thin slice from the back of each one, so that they sit evenly.
3. Spread the cream cheese into the hollows in the celery and top each one with a cold chipolata sausage.
4. Cut each of the cheese slices diagonally into 2 triangles. Cut each triangle down the middle to make 2 smaller triangles. These will form the sails.
5. Now attach each sail to its cocktail-stick mast. To do this, thread the cocktail stick through the bottom of the longest side and out again through the top of that side.
6. Carefully push the cocktail sticks into the sausages to finish the sailing boat effect.
7. Place the shredded lettuce on a serving plate and arrange the sailing boats on top.

ICE CREAM BEARS

Serves 4

INGREDIENTS	YOU WILL NEED
4 thick slices Swiss roll	sharp knife
4 scoops vanilla ice cream	4 serving plates
4 chocolate peppermint creams	ice cream scoop
8 green jelly tots (for eyes)	
4 red jelly tots	

Preparation time: 4-5 minutes

1. Arrange a slice of Swiss roll on 4 serving plates.
2. Top each one with a scoop of ice cream.
3. Cut each peppermint cream in half and press into the sides of each scoop of ice cream to form ears.
4. Decorate each scoop of ice cream with 2 green jelly tots for eyes.
5. Cut each red jelly tot in half and arrange them in an upside-down T shape to form the nose and mouth.
6. Serve at once.

TEDDY BEARS' PICK 'N' DIP

Serves 4-6

INGREDIENTS	YOU WILL NEED
1 carrot	vegetable peeler
2 spring onions	grater
100 g (4 oz) soft cream cheese	chopping board
2 tablespoons tomato ketchup	sharp knife
3 tablespoons salad cream	medium bowl
To serve:	tablespoon
2 carrots	fork
2 celery stalks	small serving bowl
12 pretzels	serving plate
1 small bag salted crisps	
6 bread sticks	

Preparation time: 25 minutes

From left to right: Teddy Bears' Pick 'n' Dip, Happy Hedgehog, Striped Double Deckers (p.57)

1. Peel and grate one carrot and chop the spring onions. Put them to one side.
2. Put the cream cheese into a medium bowl, add the tomato ketchup and the salad cream and mix them together with a fork until they are evenly combined.
3. Stir in the grated carrot and the chopped spring onions and mix well. Spoon into a small bowl.
4. Prepare the vegetable sticks for serving. Peel the 2 carrots and cut them in half lengthways. Now cut them into sticks. Trim and halve the celery stalks and cut them into narrower sticks.
5. Place the small serving bowl of dip in the middle of a serving plate and arrange the celery, carrots, pretzels, crisps and bread sticks around the bowl of dip.

HAPPY HEDGEHOG

Makes 16 nibbles

INGREDIENTS
100 g (4 oz) Cheddar
  cheese
1 × 227 (8 oz) can hotdog
  sausages
8 green grapes
8 black grapes
16 tomato wedges
1 grapefruit

YOU WILL NEED
sharp knife
chopping board
can opener
16 cocktail sticks

Preparation time: 10 minutes

1. Cut the cheese into small cubes, so that you have 16 pieces. Open the can of sausages, drain them, and cut each sausage into about 3 pieces.
2. Thread a cube of cheese, a piece of hotdog sausage and a black or green grape onto each cocktail stick.
3. Stick a small piece of tomato at the end of each one.
4. Cut a thin slice off the base of the grapefruit so that it will stand firm on a serving plate or board. Stick the cocktail sticks into the grapefruit.

GIANT OATMEAL SUNDAE

Serves 1

INGREDIENTS
1 small slice melon
6 strawberries
1 crunchy muesli bar
1 ice cream bar
a little chocolate sauce
28 g (1 oz) mixed nuts
To decorate:
1 glacé cherry or whole strawberry
1 fan wafer

YOU WILL NEED
sharp knife
chopping board
small bowl
spoon
tall sundae glass
long sundae spoon

Preparation time: 10 minutes

1. Cut the flesh of the melon into small cubes, making sure you have taken out all the seeds. Slice the strawberries. Break the muesli bar and crush it. Cut up the ice cream bar.
2. Mix the melon and the strawberries together in a bowl. Put half the fruit in a sundae glass. Sprinkle over half of the crushed muesli bar.
3. Top this with half the cubed ice cream and spoon over a little chocolate sauce.
4. Sprinkle with half of the nuts.
5. Repeat these layers again, using the remaining ingredients and finishing with a sprinkling of nuts.
6. Decorate each sundae with a glacé cherry or whole strawberry and serve with a fan wafer.

Most Teddy Bears like nothing better than snoozing in the shade on hot summer days with a glass of something refreshing near at hand. Whether you like your drinks thick and frothy, fizzy or fruity, there's a thirst-quencher here to please everyone. For a special occasion, or if you simply want to impress your friends, why not decorate your super-cool drinks with a colourful fruit kebab. Just spear a few small pieces of fruit onto a toothpick and rest it across the rim of your glass.

BANANA FROTHIES

Serves 4

INGREDIENTS
2 bananas
300 ml (½ pint) cold milk
300 ml (½ pint) plain
  yoghurt
2 tablespoons clear honey

YOU WILL NEED
knife
chopping board
measuring jug
tablespoon
blender goblet
4 medium glasses
4 straws

Preparation time: 10 minutes

1. Peel and slice the bananas and put them in the blender goblet. Add the milk, yoghurt and honey. Blend for 30-40 seconds until you have a smooth, frothy liquid. (Ask an adult to help you do this.)
2. Pour the frothy drink into 4 medium glasses and serve at once with straws.

CHOCOLATE CREAM FLOATS

Serves 4

INGREDIENTS
600 ml (1 pint) cold milk
2 tablespoons malted milk
  powder
5 tablespoons chocolate
  sauce
4 scoops chocolate or
  vanilla ice cream
4 chocolate flakes

YOU WILL NEED
measuring jug
tablespoon
blender goblet
ice cream scoop
4 medium glasses
4 straws
4 long sundae spoons

Preparation time: 10 minutes

1. Place the milk, malted milk powder and only 3 tablespoons of the chocolate sauce into the blender goblet. Blend for 30-45 seconds until mixture is thoroughly combined.
2. Pour the mixture into 4 medium-sized glasses. Add a scoop of ice cream to each glass and spoon a little of the remaining chocolate sauce over each one. Serve at once with straws and long-handled sundae spoons. Decorate each one with a chocolate flake.

■■ HONEY-POT STRAWBERRY SODAS ■■

Serves 4

Preparation time: 10 minutes

INGREDIENTS
1 × 385 g (13.6 oz) can
  strawberries
300 ml (½ pint)
  unsweetened orange juice
2 tablespoons clear honey
300 ml (½ pint) block
  raspberry ripple ice
  cream
250 ml (8 fl oz) can cream
  soda (or use fizzy lemonade)

YOU WILL NEED
can opener
blender goblet
measuring jug
tablespoon
knife
4 tall glasses
4 straws
4 long sundae spoons

1. Place the strawberries and their juice in the blender goblet. Add the orange juice and the honey and blend for 30 seconds until smooth. (Ask an adult to help you.)
2. Cut the ice cream into cubes and put half of them in the blender and blend again until smooth and frothy.
3. Pour the mixture into 4 tall glasses and add the remaining ice cream cubes to each glass. Top up each glass with cream soda or fizzy lemonade.
4. Serve at once with straws and long sundae spoons.

From left to right: Chocolate Cream Float (p.61), Banana Frothy (p.61), Honey-pot Strawberry Soda

N·O·T·E·S

N·O·T·E·S

_____

_____

_____

_____

_____

_____

_____

_____

_____

_____